PRINCIPLES OF
TEACHING SOCCER

by
Allen Wade

Published by
REEDSWAIN INC

Library of Congress Cataloging - in - Publication Data

Wade, Allen
  Teaching the Principles of Soccer

ISBN No. 1-890946-11-7
Copyright © 1997 Allen Wade
Library of Congress Catalog Card Number 97-075736

Reedswain books are available at special discounts for bulk purchase. For details contact the Special Sales Manager at Reedswain 1-800-331-5191.

Credits: Art Direction, Layout, Design and Diagrams • Kimberly N. Bender
Cover Photo: Empics

REEDSWAIN VIDEOS AND BOOKS, INC.
612 Pughtown Road • Spring City Pennsylvania 19475
1-800-331-5191

Table of Contents

Introduction 2

Chapter 1
Young Players 4

Chapter 2
The Soccer Teacher 9

Chapter 3
The Teaching and Learning Process 15

Chapter 4
Acquiring Soccer Skill 44

Chapter 5
The Game 73

Conclusion 161

Introduction

M any books have been written about soccer; almost all have concentrated on the so called basic skills of the game and on a few elementary tactical ideas. This book concentrates on the processes by which players learn to acquire those skills, how to play the game and the expertise involved in teaching them; it is for soccer TEACHERS not soccer COACHES.

Any coach worth the name should be an experienced, well trained soccer teacher before even thinking of becoming a coach: very few are.

Coaches often have to work with players whose deficiencies in basic techniques, especially in two footed techniques, seriously limit, even prohibit, their deployment in certain tactical roles. A coach has two choices: either he changes his tactics and hopes to hide those deficiencies or he corrects them: few coaches do that.

Correction requires an understanding of:
- what skill is,
- the total process of learning through teaching,
- the design and direction of effective practices.
- player development in all respects.

Soccer teachers (and coaches) should seek experience at the most primitive levels of player and skill development. Each rung in the ladder of progress may have relevance to 'new learning' for top professionals or for the youngest schoolboy. For example, any player who cannot control the ball instantly, at chest height say, has much the same learning problem as a ten year old schoolboy without the skill at all. Finding a solution may be quicker for the former but the learning process will be almost the same.

Eventually, teachers guide their pupils through situations where they learn how best to transfer technical skills and principles of play into effective match performance. This aim is long term and is the stage at which the teacher, to a limited extent, may coach. In the interim, teaching requires a high degree of perception in analyzing and building skilled movements. It is one thing to have a general idea of what a soccer technique involves, it is quite another to see precisely why and how technical errors occur and how best to put them right.

Before going any further it may be as well to say what, in my opinion, a soccer teacher should be basically concerned with. First he is in the business of increasing the range and the quality of technical options available to players. Subsequently he will teach players how, where and when to apply those techniques in combination with other players and eventually to use them to defeat opponents in defense and attack. He will educate players in the principles of soccer play and the relevance of those principles to tactical method and understanding. Match play, for a teacher, is used to assess the effectiveness of teaching and practice, not merely to achieve match results.

A teacher's role should never be confused with that of a coach, whose success (or failure) is measured exclusively almost by team results.

A soccer coach may, from time to time, teach, but strictly speaking a soccer teacher should not coach, at least not with his teaching group of players. The functions and the responsibilities of coaches and teachers are complementary but different.

One of the game's great problems is created by teachers who want to be coaches and coaches who pay lip service to the functions of teachers.

I apologize for using the expressions 'soccer teacher' and 'soccer coach', it is a serious error. Too often soccer teachers and soccer coaches teach and coach soccer: they shouldn't! Too many soccer teachers and coaches want to show how much they know about the game. Having played the game, if they have, they see coaching and teaching as processes whereby those who know tell or show those who don't; teaching and coaching are not quite that simple.

Teachers and coaches should concern themselves first and last with what players bring to the learning situation and even more importantly what they take away from it.

Chapter 1
Young Players

1.1 Natural Endowments.

Young players bring to the learning situation many different aptitudes and capacities at different stages of development. The seven year old is unquestionably different from the same player two years later, the fourteen year old almost unrecognizable from the boy of eleven or twelve.

It is dangerously easy to take any young players, within say any acceptable age 'band' and for the sake of organizational convenience treat them as if they are roughly speaking at the same stage of development: most probably they aren't. Age is no indication of what players are capable of and 'banding' (the bringing together of players who seem to be in similar 'age stages' of development) is no more than a rough and ready convenience.

In diagram 1, I have listed ten developmental characteristics of great importance to a teacher. The strength or weakness of each characteristic is classified on a scale of one to five during each developmental stage. These assessments are out of my own experience and a distillation of some work done by child psychologists in observing behavioral development. The evaluation of their significance to teachers are mine and are no more than guides. If they only make soccer teachers look at players with greater discernment they are justified.

1.2 Development Stages and Banding.

Banding is the bringing together of players in groups irrespective of their specific ages on the basis of similarities in development; age alone is a poor indication of anything in human development. Young people may be seven years of age 'physically', nine 'verbally', eight in 'numeracy' and eleven in 'soccer'. Soccer players, subject to hugely influential environmental influences, may defy any attempt to categorize them in relation to this age or that. I have seen players, ten or eleven years of age, with a 'sense' of the game in some ways superior to that shown by some professionals. A 'sense' of the game is what seems to be an instinctive awareness of what is going on.

In fact, game sense is not instinctive. It is learned out of a deep and sustained commitment to soccer play and practice.

Any skill acquired through self teaching can be taught; there is no such thing as a born soccer player.

It is sometimes convenient organizationally and motivationally to bring young players together for certain forms of teaching and practice IF the groups are small enough to enable effective individual teaching to take place.

In diagram 1, where young players show similar characteristics of development they may be taught together. For example, nine and ten year olds seem to show high levels of co-ordination and skillfulness and also early responsiveness to small group tactical practice. These young players may be brought together with advantages to both 'year' groups. The older players practice with players less mature in some respects who may provide less severe practice opposition. The younger players, with similar levels of skill, will be tested by exposing their skills to more mature co-operation and opposition. Of course, over-exposure to significantly superior opponents, in play or in practice, may seriously blunt the ambition and the skill of players less well endowed. Conversely, excessive exposure of skillful players to sustained play and practice with significantly less skillful players will retard the development of the former.

Sustained commitments to league and cup competitions for all players between say seven and fourteen years may seriously retard skill development.

When young players only play for results, they quickly learn what they can't do and their ambition and imagination is blunted. They become functional rather than imaginative.

Highly skillful, clever players are bred out of long experiences of trial and success, not trial and failure.

Personal experience of banding led me to the following conclusions. Seven year olds with eights seemed workable as did nines with ten year olds. Strangely eight year olds grouped with nine year olds were not so successful in my experience. Because of England's educational system at the time I was unable to evaluate the banding of tens and elevens but eleven year olds with twelves worked satisfactorily other than where a pre-adolescence growth spurt occurred with some extra-mature twelve year olds. The competitiveness of eleven year olds and the reaction of the twelves towards it needed strict teacher control; both ages, shall we say, tend to be combative.

Acceleration into adolescence in the thirteen to fourteen 'age' group, exemplified by some considerable growth spurts, made banding between them difficult. Adolescence seemed to me to warrant a quite separate treatment in the soccer teaching situation.

Fifteen year olds and sixteens were compatible and worked well together competitively and in practice; both age groups seemed balanced and mature.

Sixteen year old players who are usually well developed in physique and in skill are commonly accepted as apprentice professionals in England. The outstanding ones practice frequently with and against young, full profes-

Scale
1= Very Low
5 = very high

AGES AND STAGES

DEVELOPMENTAL CHARACTERISTICS	5 +/-	6 +/-	7 +/-	8 +/-	9 +/-	10 +/-	11 +/-	12 +/-	13 +/-	14 +/-	15 +/-	16 +/-	
SKILLFULNESS AND CO-ORDINATION	5	2	3	4	4	5	4	3	2	3	4	5	1
COMMITMENT TO SOLO PRACTICE	1	1	3	2	4	3	2	3	3	4	3	2	2
COMMITMENT TO GROUP PRACTICE	1	2	2	3	4	5	5	5	4	5	4	4	3
COMMITMENT TO TEACHER DIRECTION	4	3	3	2	3	5	4	3	4	4	3	5	4
COMPETITIVENESS	5	4	3	2	1	3	5	4	4	3	4	5	5
QUARRELSOMENESS	1	5	3	2	1	1	3	2	4	3	2	1	6
SELF CRITICAL	1	1	3	4	4	3	2	3	4	4	2	2	7
REACTION TO CRITICISM	1	5	5	2	1	1	2	2	4	3	4	4	8
PRAISE DEMANDING	3	5	3	2	2	2	3	3	4	3	2	1	9
RESPONSE TO LEADERSHIP	3	2	2	4	3	4	5	3	2	4	4	5	10

Diagram 1. *The development characteristics of young players.*

sionals, sometimes unwisely. Sixteen, seventeen and eighteen year olds can be taught, practice and play together easily and beneficially.

The bands to which I have referred here cater for all young players other than the exceptionally advanced and the exceptionally backward player. Advanced players are easily accommodated in any teaching arrangement because practices can be weighted to make their problems greater than those for the less gifted.

It is difficult to accommodate backward young players other than among those of a similar standard. Backward players benefit enormously from occasional practice and play with a few of the best players. Gifted players, with the right attitude to joint practice, can significantly inspire those less gifted.

Gifted youngsters in any walk of life must always receive special consideration: they are a rare and valuable species.

1.3 Hot Housing.

This is the deliberately accelerated development given to selected, outstanding players. It is derived from the carefully controlled and contrived treatment and growing conditions given to exotic plants in hot houses. Some soccer players respond to hot housing well, others react against it, sometimes fiercely; its effects should be watched carefully. Early acceptance of special provision and status is no guarantee that development will be assured and predictable. It is the attitudes of young players towards other players, towards the intensity of commitment to practice, training and to play upon which development and progress depend. Many outstanding young players find the expectations to which early promise gives rise intolerable; they react against it. Some players regard high expectations as unacceptable demands upon their freedom; they may be right. Even parents can be surprised by the strength of the reaction against 'hyped' expectations.

In England, in 1964, I persuaded The Football Association to set up The National Football School; it came into being twenty years later. Two years residential education and specialized soccer teaching were offered to thirty two boys between fourteen and sixteen years of age. A normal school curriculum was supplemented by daily, two hour practice and teaching sessions. A number of professional clubs, some of whose schoolboy soccer coaching programs bordered on child abuse, criticized the concept as over-protective, inflexible, robotic and excessively intense! The only criticism I made was that starting serious soccer teaching at fourteen was wildly optimistic. Soccer players show the 'signs' of exceptional talent nearer to five years of age than to fifteen. Most of the world class players within my personal knowledge taught themselves the basic and the extraordinary personal skills upon which greatness is built. The single most important and common factor was their commitment, in some cases obsession, to becoming as skillful as human nature, play and practice could make them.

Hot housing the gifted is as much a matter of knowing when not to teach as knowing what to teach. Self-taught players commonly speak of practice and play commitments of six or more hours each day. Given that sort of interest and ready access to players, first class teachers should short circuit and accelerate the learning and development process significantly.

Soccer teaching. . . gifted soccer teaching. . . minimizes learning errors while opening a pupil's mind to barely imaginable possibilities. That sort of hot housing requires not only exceptional playing potential, it requires teaching talent of the very highest order, far beyond the capabilities of most volunteer teachers in schools or outside them. Certainly way beyond the capabilities of schoolboy soccer coaches at professional clubs in England, many of whom rarely teach even the game's basics acceptably.

Hot housing involves the careful and progressive, occasionally regressive, exposure to all the conceivable circumstances in which a player may be required to be skillful. The highest levels at which soccer skills must be executed are developed out of supreme player confidence.

Confidence comes from sustained, successful experience at levels which expose the player to challenge but not to levels of challenge with which he has difficulty in coping.

The strength of the opposition to which gifted players should be subjected, in or outside a hot house, must be adjusted carefully; there is no guarantee that progress will always be onward and upward.

Chapter 2
The Soccer Teacher

W hat do players expect from soccer teachers: what are their most important characteristics: what are the skills and the attributes needed by effective soccer teachers? What are the personality traits and areas of expertise upon which we could begin to select and educate expert soccer teachers for the future?

2.1 Players' Expectations.

(a) Young players want to be taught how, where and when to 'do' things 'better' on the soccer field.

Doing things 'better' may mean being more successful in play and practice with and against other players. Doing things 'better' may mean getting more approval from people whose opinions, rightly or wrongly, count. What the player perceives as better may not be totally compatible with what a teacher sees as better. Their views have to be reconciled. Teachers often have to 'give way' in the interests of achieving longer term objectives.

(b) Young players want to be taught to be as clever (tricky) as the best players in their group.

And the best players want to be taught to be even trickier than they are: no easy task for even exceptional teachers.

(c) Young players (and not so young ones for that matter) want to know how they are rated in the eyes of people they perceive as being experts and they need to know their ratings frequently.

Soccer teachers come into the category of experts. . . for as long as they can persuade players that they are experts!

(d) Players expect to be taught how to deal with problems which embarrass them when playing with and against other players.

(e) Players expect practice and teaching situations to be as exciting as play itself. If they aren't, teachers may find their teaching groups diminishing, rapidly.

(f) Young players expect soccer teachers to be aware of all of their problems and to find solutions for them. The higher up the skill ladder we climb the less sure some of us are.

Teachers provide reassurance and rebuild confidence in using soccer skill, at best a fragile commodity.

(g) Finally, players need a teacher's support in gaining and holding onto 'peer' approval. Players need recognition for what they are and for what they achieve, not only from their teachers but almost as importantly from their teammates; it's called respect.

2.2 Personality.

It is not, in my view, possible to implement a successful strategy for soccer development without addressing the problem of teacher and coach selection, training and appointment. Teaching and coaching appointments should only be made upon real potential. Assumed 'know how' based upon playing experience is likely to be more illusory than real. And the willingness of volunteers is a guarantee of nothing other than. . . willingness.

Too many people become soccer teachers who need the job more than the job needs them.

There must be minimal playing experience but teaching and coaching success depend much more on personality and applied intelligence than on soccer skill. 'Personality', as I use the term, is the impression which teachers create in order to exert influence on others. The best teachers appear to have certain 'natural' qualifications for success in the job although the extent to which they are entirely 'natural' is questionable.

Not only are there no born soccer players, there are no born teachers.

(a) Leadership.

People with significant powers of leadership tend to be more successful in the teaching situation than those without.

Leaders are reckoned to have some or all of the following characteristics:

1. They command respect from all or most of any group.
2. They take decisions: even unpleasant ones.
3. Leaders have a confident assertiveness and inspirational enthusiasm for getting a job done.
4. Good leaders are honest and fair.
5. They have reliable analytical and problem solving capacities. They come up with the right answers.
6. Leaders are hard working.
7. They are receptive to ideas and have a shrewd, open mindedness.
8. Leaders are temperamentally stable, especially under pressure.
9. Most leaders are sound organizers and planners.
10. Leaders are ambitious for their own and for their group's success.

I would place those characteristics in that order of importance; others might attach different degrees of importance but I would not expect argument about the inclusion of any item on the list.

(b) Painstaking.
Good teachers take care. They can and do improvise but only on the basis of sound preparation and planning. They are:
1. Thoughtful.
2. Deliberate and controlled.
3. Prepared to take the details of a situation into account.
4. Good at anticipating problems.

(c) Initiative.
1. Effective teachers are rarely put off or surprised by apparently unforeseen circumstances.
2. They have a willingness to try new approaches in solving difficult problems.

(d) Persistence.
1. First class teachers show high perseverance in tackling problems; they are determined to see the job through to the end.
2. They have a capacity for inspiring others to sustain their efforts even under extreme difficulties.

(e) Sociability.
The best teachers know that players want and need lives outside soccer; teachers are not obsessive. They show a very broad appreciation of all aspects of their players' personal and social circumstances.

(f) Humor.
Teaching and learning can become hyper-intensive. Intensity can destroy confidence, especially among the young and immature.

Expectations become overwhelming and outstanding teachers use humor to reduce pressure on young players but only rarely and very carefully at a player's expense.

2.3 Personal Attributes and Skills.
Teaching is a practical matter, not a theoretical exercise; academic institutions responsible for educating teachers, in all disciplines, have tried to turn it into one. Doing so has been of little benefit to the profession, to the practice of teaching or to those at the receiving end.

There are certain ways of going about any form of teaching which, while not guaranteeing success, will pay: other ways may create more problems than they solve.

(a) Appearance.

The first impact made by a soccer teacher is at first sight. A teacher's style of dress, personal appearance and physical bearing is either worth a second look, non-descript or trashy. If it is the first all well and good; if the second, the teacher himself may be judged as non-descript before he even opens his mouth; if it is the third, he may have seriously handicapped himself. A soccer teacher's dress and appearance should reflect his intention to set standards, to work purposefully and to seem worthy of imitation.

Of course it is possible to overdo anything, to be extravagantly impressive in appearance. 'Putting on too much style' may cause players' expectations of a new teacher to ascend to impossible levels. Let the players down and they will let the teacher down. However, if a teacher wants his group to take pride in their appearance and thereby in their performances he must lead from the front.

Without pride, players are likely to be short on self respect: without self respect they are unlikely to develop respect for anything or for anybody, least of all anyone in charge of them.

Looking 'the part' is worth working at; it is a skill and can be learned.

(b) Manner and Voice.

The next most impressive impact factor after a teacher's appearance is what he says and how he says it. Soccer teachers are expected to be superior beings: most of us are! Not only should we look superior we should sound superior. Teachers must learn to think before they speak. They must decide what needs to be said and at least as importantly how they are going to say it. Being very sparing with what is said gains time to think about what needs to be said next. In soccer, thinking time is best gained by giving the players something to do, preferably something challenging, and by keeping them 'at' it.

Working outdoors, there may be a tendency to shout: it should be resisted. The ability to 'lift and throw' one's voice is an important skill but dangerous when used excessively.

A teacher's voice should be used like a musical instrument, to create expression and impression, not merely to make a noise.

The quieter a coach is the more his players will strain to hear what he has to say, if what he has to say is worth listening to. If it isn't, he should keep quiet!

Soccer players are inquisitive. . . some might say 'nosey'. . . by nature. If they think that something is being said from which they are being excluded, they will move heaven and earth to hear it.

Break the connection between listening and learning and it is difficult to re-establish; the connection is called interest.

An extensive vocabulary allows the use of words which, in themselves, command attention and interest: they enable a teacher to 'paint word pictures'. Unusual words, used sparingly, provoke inquiry and interest. However, coaching and teaching jargon, 'buzz words' used to distinguish those 'in the know' from those less fortunate, are dangerous. They are used to create a sense of superiority; more often than not they become pretentious; they should be avoided.

Players need teachers to tell them what to do and how to do it and showing them is preferable to telling them every time.

(c) Impressionism.

Impressionists are actors capable of impersonating other people and their various moods. Teachers should try to develop impressionist skills. Fundamental to effective teaching is the ability to affect the attitudes of players towards what is being taught. Soccer teachers who can convincingly 'turn on' different moods to suit the actions and reactions of players in the teaching situation have considerable power at their disposal. The skill requires self discipline and a lot of practice. Overdone and a teacher can lose respect, but the skill is particularly important when he has to take players to task for unacceptable behavior, or attitudes, or when he seeks to 'lift' the performance of players who are, for one reason or another, despondent. Acting is also a learned skill: improving it will pay considerable dividends.

(d) Teacher: Player Relationships.

Teaching is rarely as straight forward as teachers or players would wish. Circumstances change and the attitudes of players are affected by many factors outside the teacher's immediate control and often outside his knowledge. School pupils, college students and certainly many soccer players try to neutralize a teacher's authority by seeking familiar relationships. Once established, familiarity is difficult to change into the sometimes distant, critical, judgmental and even authoritarian relationship needed when misbehavior or willfully unsatisfactory performance have to be castigated.

Successful and respected teachers, and it's hardly conceivable that a teacher could be successful without respect, keep their players at a distance most of the time. They allow degrees of friendliness to emerge occasionally but familiarity, never. Players should never be one hundred percent certain what a teacher's reaction will be to border-line behavior: better on the cold side of cool than over-friendly.

Most of the better coaches and teachers, within my experience, wear permanent expressions of weary skepticism or outright disbelief whenever they see players approaching with what they anticipate to be requests for special consideration. It's easy to soften one's attitude as circumstances dictate; it's difficult to harden it.

The assumption that players are only too ready to 'try things on' with people in authority is a safer starting point than one of trust. Assume that players are always trying to put one over on you and your defenses at least will be in place; they need to be.

2.4 Relevant Areas of Knowledge.
This book is about the practice of soccer teaching. It is not intended to provide a comprehensive curriculum for training soccer teachers.

Nevertheless, it may be of some help to indicate those subject areas some knowledge of which would be of significant help in their training or in their advanced education:

    (a) Child Development.
    (b) Anatomy, Physiology and Human Kinetics.
    (c) The Psychology of Skill Acquisition.
    (d) The Theory and Practice of Physical Education and Sports Training.
    (e) The Practical and Ethical Significance of The Laws of The Game.
    (f) The Principles of Attack and Defense and of Individual Play.

Chapter 3
The Teaching
and Learning Processes

3.1 The Art of Teaching.

A soccer player's idea of success depends upon a broad agreement between himself, anyone who influences his perception of the game outside the teaching situation and his teacher. This agreement may be tacit between teacher and player, but the involvement of a third party, particularly a very influential one, a parent say, may need negotiation. The teacher plays a dominant part in the formulation of ideas and ideals of what individual and team play should try to become. Clearly, how teams play is inextricably bound up with what the capabilities are of individual players within them. In senior soccer the coach has the ultimate sanction of replacing players who can't or won't contribute to team strategy. It will pay teachers and coaches to go about the business of change on the basis of consensus. Imposing new concepts of style and strategy may seem necessary in certain circumstances, especially for coaches, but without broad agreement it is unlikely to offer long term possibilities.

The soccer teacher's art is:
- first, in persuading young players of the attractiveness of different styles of play:
- second, of the need and the possibilities for them to develop and expand their own individual capabilities and
- third, motivating them towards a commitment to change in performance which will reinforce their belief in one and two.

Persuasion will be founded on the teachers' ability to enable players to 'see themselves' as they are and, with his help, as they should aim to become.

The soccer teacher is in the business of inspiring young players to have a clear vision of the game as an exercise in skill and in applied intelligence. Consequently his main objective will be to help each player to develop his individual potentialities to the highest possible level: ultimately for the good of whatever team he eventually plays for. Many players have been seriously disillusioned when, having been brought up in one soccer 'faith', they find themselves playing for teams with totally different ideals.

English soccer's soul searching, prevalent since the game's decline, has never acknowledged the extent to which many outstanding schoolboy players, taught to pursue technical excellence and cleverness, found themselves in professional clubs in which physical power and size together with kick and chase doctrines were everything: the exact antithesis of all that they had been taught during the most formative years of their soccer lives. Many never recovered from the devastating blow to their beliefs. Clubs privileged to have access to technically excellent players must, when they emerge, encourage them to play technically excellent soccer. When senior soccer's playing styles and beliefs are incompatible with what teachers are teaching, the teaching process, top to bottom, becomes ridiculous.

Inspiration and teaching based on a game that doesn't exist is likely to bring about player and teacher disillusion of a disastrous order: in England it did.

Having established a 'beach head' between himself and his group, having drawn behavioral demarcation lines, a soccer teacher should be as warm, friendly, constructively critical and as understanding in manner as circumstances require and allow. Hectoring, crudely aggressive, hostile, intolerant teachers are almost contradictions in themselves.

The players will show a teacher how far he may safely go in any direction. An effective teacher will be the major influence within the playing group without seeming to be. He will create a mutually respectful practice atmosphere. His contribution will be firm, informed but not overwhelming; his effectiveness comes out of leading, persuading and finally convincing rather than from ranting and raving.

Over-dominant teachers (and coaches) talk too much, too loudly and too often. They give orders, ignore attempts to contribute by others and listen with pained intolerance whenever they are offered. And I apologize here and now!

Over-dominant soccer teachers rarely initiate discussion. They state their inflexible positions often aggressively and with no room for argument. This condition is increasingly common among schoolboy and youth soccer coaches; it indicates feelings of inadequacy within them; they. . . the coaches that is. . . should be avoided.

The art of teaching in many ways is a matter of knowing when not to. Effective teaching occurs when players are motivated towards improvement through change and with reasonable expectations of achieving it. Teachers should stay out of learning situations until intervention is needed and preferably asked for; too few understand this.

3.2 Teaching Methods.
3.21 Target Teaching.
Soccer teaching should be as objective as it can be; much more than it ever is. Objectivity is a matter of setting and achieving targets. A soccer

teacher should have a detailed 'map' of soccer development for each of his players. The map should indicate where the players, individually and collectively, are and will be at the beginning, during and towards the end of the development process. At the end they should be well prepared for entry into competitive soccer.

The map should indicate clearly the 'milestones' by which progress will be or has been measured. A professional soccer teacher will actually record, on the map if possible, the magnitude and significance of the causes of progression or regression. The players should know the master plan: what it entails: what its implications are for them: where they are on it at any given time and how they are likely to progress to the next mile-stone. 'Third parties' to the development of young players, parents and other relatives say, must be brought into development discussions and their co-operation sought.

Teachers can teach but only players can practice, often alone or at best with the help of someone other than the teacher. Everyone must steer by the same compass, if you'll excuse the nautical metaphor.

Teaching by objectives involves the following considerations:
(a) A starting point.
A detailed appraisal of where exactly the player is in development.

(b) Time.
Progress cannot be haphazard. Everyone needs to know how long each stage of progress should take and whether or not it has been achieved in the planned time. If it hasn't the plan must be altered to accommodate new time scales.

(c) Progress Markers. (milestones)
Players need to know what they are trying to achieve and the extent to which they have achieved it. Objectives must be reasonable and attain-able. When they are unattainable or very difficult motivation is destroyed.

(d) Agreement of Intentions.
The teacher should set down what is expected of everyone involved and seek their agreement to that statement.

(e) Resources.
Without suitable and adequate resources teaching will fail.
If, for example, a unit of teaching and practice needs one ball to every two players, impossible problems are created if only two balls are available for the whole squad. An expert teacher might 'make do' once or twice but only at the expense of progress and enthusiasm.

(f) Monitoring.
The methods and frequency by which progress will be monitored should be agreed upon.

(g) Support.
The agreement of third parties or other 'assistants' should be sought. Agreeing to one process but following another undermines the teaching process and the authority of the teacher.

(h) Recognition.
From time to time and by prior arrangement, everyone involved should come together for mutual 'back slapping', a process by which each participant's contribution is given recognition. Achievement can be rewarded by seemingly trivial, even comical prizes. Too much prize quality and cost can be a 'knock down' for those not receiving anything; ideally everyone should receive something, however insignificant.

Rewards are never insignificant to those who receive them.

I know of experienced international players, earning astronomical salaries, who have stood up with pride to receive 'best practice player of the day' awards. . . a red apple or a bar of chocolate, both beautifully wrapped of course! Teachers and coaches should never underestimate players' appreciation of awards, even those given for trying hard but failing! And players should never assume that teachers or coaches are immune to appreciation. We are all in the recognition and reward business: in sport, exceptionally so.

3.3 Preparation.
Knowing where to go and agreeing how best to get there without adequate resources will be to no avail. Equipment and apparatus suitable in size and in number is the only basis for individual development or small group interplay. Left alone, young players in Third World countries produce themselves out of the most unlikely practice conditions, mostly at the expense of school and any other activity likely to take up some of their time.

Where those sorts of huge daily time commitments aren't possible, teachers have to short cut the development process. But the best soccer teachers in the world will not 'talk' young players into improvement. . . at least not of any lasting significance. If players are to be taught during winter nights, floodlit outdoor areas or sizable indoor facilities have to be accessed, preferably the former.

No access, no practice, no progress!

(a) Practice Space.

Space needed for teaching should be calculated on the basis of 100 - 200 square yards per player. The more skillful a group the less the square yardage needed; the less skillful, the greater the need for space.

Space equals time in soccer and without space or time, or both, players cannot learn or use skill.

12 players need an area 40 yds x 30 or 40 yds x 60.

16 players need an area 40 yds x 40 or 40 yds x 80.

18 players need an area 60 yds x 30 or 60 yds x 60.

Goalkeepers are not counted unless they are committed to 'out of penalty area' practice to a significant extent.

(b) Soccer Balls.

Effective technical and basic tactical practices require a minimum ball to player ratio of one to three. Any lower ball to player ratio and a teacher must produce a practice to accommodate the ball shortage rather than an effective learning situation. And the ball sizes should suit the physical and skill capabilities of the players.

(c) Portable Goals.

Without goals of some kind, shooting practice loses its excitement. Shooting and scoring are the life blood of the game in practice or in competition; most (I am tempted to say all) young player practices should end with a shot at goal whatever the practice's main objective.

(d) Practice Vests.

Distinguishing colors make player identification easier and practice that much more easily directed.

(e) Area Markers.

Ground markers (cones), brightly colored, half domes made of synthetic, rubberoid material, no less than 4" in diameter, enable a teacher to change practice space and shape to meet specific practice objectives. Practicing in unrestricted space is unrealistic to the players and reduces any chance of control by the teacher.

In England, players' lack of technical skill is often put down to imperfect practice grounds which are less than perfectly level, bumpy, badly drained or where the grass is upwards of ankle deep.

Most of the world's great players, almost all self taught, practiced and played on surfaces where a predictable bounce simply wasn't!

Sensitivity of touch comes from extremely late adjustments of technique. Unpredictability of bounce or 'run' forces players to develop extra sensitive ' feel' for the ball and late touch.

(f) Rebound Boards.
Vertical rebound walls or boards four feet high and six or eight feet long are useful but not vital.

(g) Diving and Jumping Pits or Mattresses.
Aerial work for goalkeepers and other players who may have to produce aerial gymnastic skills is made more acceptable by the accessibility of large, soft, sand pits or gymnastic mattresses. Sooner or later of course, realistic practice has to take place in realistic conditions.

There are many other pieces of equipment, some of it highly ingenious, produced to assist in soccer training and practice . In recent years designing novel training and practice equipment has become a major growth industry in the world of sports equipment production. Some of it has little if any relevance to the development of more skillful players. The question to ask is, 'Does the equipment help to produce REALISTIC practice conditions or is it just curious?'

3.31 Teaching Units.
The development 'map' has already been mentioned: ideally its objectives should encompass development objectives covering at least one year (or season), for very young players, preferably two.

Medium term objectives should cover half a year or season.

Short term objectives should occupy units of teaching and practice lasting a month, at most six weeks, depending on the number of teaching sessions in a week.

A six week unit will have the same objectives in each session although in the interest of interest. . . if you know what I mean. . . certain activities may be changed. The activity may change but the objective at which the original activity was aimed remains the same.

Boredom is the arch enemy of learning. In most circumstances soccer teachers will not be able to work with their players more than three or four times each week, often only once or twice. The fewer the teaching sessions, the greater the 'homework' to be done by the player. Teachers will have to spend as much time preparing players for unsupervised practice as in direct teaching. Objectives, in these conditions, must be crystal clear and totally accepted by all parties involved. That is why teacher support courses for parents and other committed parties are very important.

3.32 Evaluation.
Tests of progress are important: whether or not they should be concrete is debatable. A perceptive teacher. . . and anyone who isn't perceptive shouldn't be one. . . notices and mentally records what he or she 'sees' all the time but mental records are not so easily recalled as those set down

in more substantial forms; the two should go together.

If they aren't, a teacher may 'record' the performances of a few players rather than all at any one time. Over a long period this may work out all right but short and medium term it may make motivation through recognition and reward that much less effective and as I have said, teachers 'live or die' by motivation.

A simple record sheet will suffice. The 'scores' need only be as accurate as the teacher's judgment skill will allow. Whenever consultation with players takes place as it must, regularly, the scores will be arguable and changeable. Records serve the purpose of focusing the minds of players, teachers and others and of motivating them to keep objectives clear in their minds.

As progress is made so the development objectives become more specific and detailed. Practice and teaching move on from technical skills and their isolated or one versus one effectiveness, to the application of those skills in small groups - twos, threes and eventually fours and fives, to defeat one and progressively more opposing practice players.

The record sheet will be expanded to include these developmental 'mile stones'. Diagram 2, page 25.

3.33 Preparing A Teaching Session.
Pre Lesson.

(a) Know exactly how many players will take part and check that they will make the starting time.

(b) Players must know what personal kit will be needed, track suit, shirt, shorts etc., soccer shoes (studded or /and 'flats'): check that the players do know.

(c) Ensure the availability of the space needed at the time needed.

(d) Check that any special markings needed on the teaching area are there.

(e) Ensure that all the equipment needed is readily available and in the required condition: balls inflated etc.

(f) If teaching assistants are involved make sure that they know exactly what their contributions will be before, during and after the session. There's nothing worse for people expecting to contribute positively, than being given demeaning, 'thought up at the last moment' tasks: it's insulting.

(g) Finally and most important of all, in the unavoidable absence of the teacher, almost certainly he's died, capable cover must have been arranged.

TECHNIQUES	DATE	FOOT		SCORE
		L.	R.	
STOPPING: GROUND PASS				
STOPPING: AERIAL PASS				
DELIVERY: GROUND PASS				
DELIVERY: VOLLEY				
DELIVERY: 1/2 VOLLEY				
DRIBBLING				
SHOOTING: GROUND				
SHOOTING: VOLLEY				
SHOOTING: 1/2 VOLLEY				
TRACKING				
INTERCEPTION				
HEADING: GENERAL				
HEADING AND JUMP				
GOALKEEPING - POSITIONING				
GOALKEEPING - FIELDING & CATCHING				
GOALKEEPING - DEFLECTING				
GOALKEEPING - PUNCHING				
DIVING TO SAVE				
DIVING TO SAVE AT FEET				
KICKING				
THROWING				

Diagram 2. *A skill record sheet.*

Teachers and coaches can be very protective of their positions. One of their most important functions is to take on the in-service training of other would-be teachers and coaches. There are few pleasures greater than seeing a young player become a sophisticated and skillful player. Perhaps one is seeing and hearing a former teaching 'apprentice' 'come good' with his or her own group of players.

There are no secrets in teaching and coaching soccer which warrant the mystery with which some coaches surround themselves. More often than not raising barriers of mystique is a sign of deep rooted feelings of insecurity or inadequacy; there's more of it about than you might think!

3.332 The Lesson. (90 minutes)

A teaching session will have a beginning, a middle and an end.

The beginning will include the warm-up, a stretching routine and the introduction.

Mature young players should know a warm-up routine and carry it out eventually without teacher supervision, other than of the most apparently casual kind. It is in 'casual', seemingly disinterested observation of players that teachers often gain useful insights into players' attitudes and personalities.

(a) Warm-Up (10 minutes)
(b) Introductory Activity (1) (10 minutes)

The introduction involves organized, self-imposed practice of known skills and techniques. The teacher nominates the skills to be practiced but needn't direct it. His occasional comments are likely to be as much motivational and humorous as informative; it's called 'winding up' the players!

'Free choice' activities may seem like a good idea but many players left to choose can't or won't: some prefer to chat. 'Chatterers' should be discouraged, positively!

(c) Introductory Activity (2) (10 minutes)

Now the teacher takes full control.

This is likely to be a repeat of a main development phase carried over from the previous week. That work is revised and key points re-emphasized.

(d) Development Phase 1. (15 minutes)

The teacher introduces another technical option associated with the theme which was designed to run through the whole of this unit of development.

(e) Development Phase 2. (15 minutes)

As previously but the teacher concentrates on linking the previous technique to another as would be required in the game. e.g. a passing option based on a controlling technique.

Soccer techniques are never employed singly, they are always part of a skill sequence; the game itself is a string of skills e.g. Control to pass, or fake a pass, or to dribble and so on.

(f) Development Phase 3. (15 minutes)
Here the group takes part in 'conditioned' game form practice of the skills treated in the previous phases.

End Phase. (5 minutes approx)
In pairs or threes players practice to achieve combined techniques scores: the technical problems set by the teacher.

The following is an example of lesson preparation in the context of a unit of work. The players might be from seven to nine years of age. The unit of work is concerned with:
    (1) The acceptance and control of aerial passes or bounces.
    (2) Control of the ball in the air and the secondary options open to players in different phases of play.
    (3) The development of deception, together with dribbling and shooting possibilities, from improved control.

Previous work involved the general skill of bringing passes under control on the ground by relaxing and pulling back the stopping surface and absorbing the force of the pass.

(a) Introduction 1.
In pairs, the players inter-pass.
The receiving player must control (trap) the ball to make his return pass possible in the fewest number of touches, ideally second touch.
- Or he must control the ball with one foot to enable him to pass with the other.
- Or he must control with one foot and pass with the same foot.
- Or he must pass with teacher nominated surfaces of the foot.

(b) Introduction 2.
In fours, A passes to B who must control the ball and pass to C or back to A before D can challenge. B, C and A inter-pass to achieve a target sequence of, say, five passes. D cannot move to challenge until B has touched the ball for the first time. B cannot kick or pass the ball with his first touch.

* **Teaching points:**
  (1) Introduce the possibility of 'shaping' to pass to one player while turning away to pass to another.
  (2) 'Shape' to pass and turn away to dribble clear of a challenge.

(c) Development 1.
In pairs, 3-5 yards apart, A throws underarm and above head height to B who tries to catch the ball on his chest or on his thigh.

* **Teaching Points:**
  (1) Emphasize relaxation and withdrawal of the stopping surface and secondary control with the foot.
  (2) Introduce catching the ball on the instep, same principles. . . relax surface and withdraw it just before impact.

The receiving player will then control the service in the air and make a ground pass back to the server with the fewest number of touches, ultimately only two.

(d) Development 2.
In threes, as in the diagram 3, A throws to B who must control the ball in the air and bring it down. C may challenge for the ball when the ball touches the ground. After bringing the ball to ground, B can shoot to score through either of the two goals. B can inter-pass with A but only B can score.

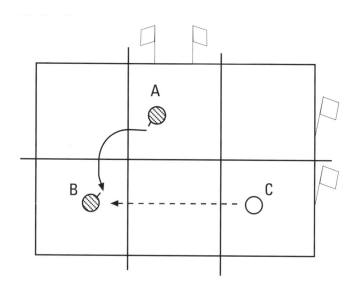

Diagram 3. *Development 2.*

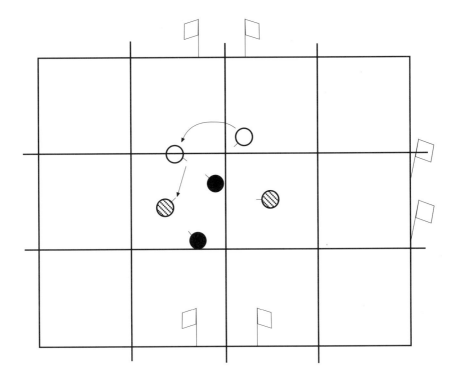

Diagram 4. *Development 3.*

(e) Development 3.
In an area 40 yards x 30 yards there are two teams of two with an extra two who always play for the team which has the ball i.e. which is attacking. This produces 4 v 2 contests. Diagram 4.
A team in possession of the ball tries to inter-pass to score.

Conditions:
(1) The ball must be thrown by one player, controlled by a receiving player before it touches the ground and passed to a third.
(2) The third player must pick up the ball and throw it to a teammate to repeat the sequence of throw, control, pass, pick up and throw.
(3) Goals may be scored only with headers.

(f) End Activity.
One ball between two players. The players practice throw, control in the air and pass sequences using the minimum of controlling touches before passing. Having controlled the ball the player must move it away from the receiving position as quickly as possible.

There is no reason why there should be two introductory phases or three development phases. However, only highly motivated young players sustain concentration for much longer than twenty minutes on one activity. If one development phase is planned to occupy the fifty minutes available, the activity upon which development is based should be adaptable to changes every twenty minutes or so even though the development objective remains unchanged.

Lesson 2.

This is for older players, 14 to 15 years.
Previous work has been on 'penetration', the ability to counter attack accurately and quickly through and behind opposing defenses.
Passing practices concentrated on ground passing skills and inter-passing possibilities created out of dribbling runs at defenders.

Number of players: 18, one or two of whom are goalkeepers.
Soccer balls: 6
Practice areas: half a full playing pitch or 60 yds x 70 - 80 yds.
Practice Goals: 4
Ground marking discs.

The objective of the lesson is to open players' minds to the possibility for using space over defenders with precision and deception.

The techniques involved are:

(1) Chipping the ball to obtain optimum height over short distances.

(2) Using back spin to 'hold' the ball on landing.

(3) 'Seeing' different running angles to meet chipped passes behind defenders.

(a) Warm-Up.

7 v 2 'keep ball' played in each half of the practice area.

A goalkeeper will use only goalkeeping skills.
The 'seven' try to complete a target number of consecutive passes before the two in the middle either intercept or are changed.
Only ground passes may be used. Alternatively the player with the ball may choose to run it at an opponent looking for a teammate with whom to set up an inter-passing move to get behind one or more defenders.
Progression: Reduce the practice to 6 v 3 and perhaps to 5 v 4.

Set new objectives:

- A completed pass between two opponents scores 1 point.
- A completed pass over an opponent(s) scores three points.
- A pass which runs out of the playing area loses two points.

More mature players should have the range of skills and the soccer 'know how' to see the possibilities available with better aerial passing skills. In fact they have been drawn into finding out for themselves, a sound basis for teaching anyone anything.

The warm up moves become the introduction naturally and the lesson can now proceed into:

(a) Development Phase 1.

In threes, A plays a short, ground pass to B who hits a lofted pass to C 30 yards away, A may move across the line of B's pass but doesn't try to interfere with it. A then turns and runs towards C. C controls the ball and plays a pass to A who returns it along the ground to C. C repeats the lofted pass to B about 30 yards away and A repeats the moves he made previously.

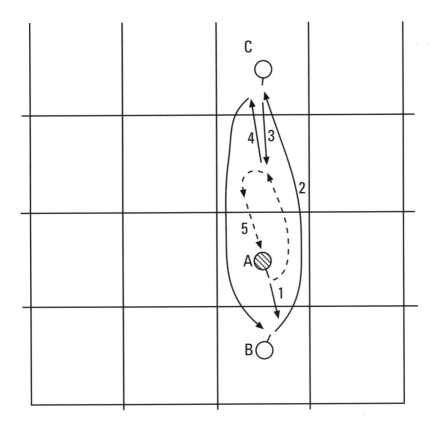

Diagram 6. *'End to end' lofted passing: perceptual (technical) practice. Passing to clear the 20 yard mid-zone.*

As practice proceeds the outside players should move a yard or two closer to each other for every repetition. The reduced distances compel players to seek greater 'loft' in their passes to 'clear' the middle player.

* Teaching points:
  (1) Strike the ball as far beneath its bottom surface as the ground will allow.
  (2) Leg swing comes from a fast extension of the knee rather than from the hip as it does in long, lofted passing.
  (3) The ball should be set up well to one side of the intended line of pass so that the kicking foot is swung round the ball rather than almost straight at it.
  (4) Follow through depends on how much distance is required, the kicking ankle is not held as firmly as for a long, lofted pass.

(b) Development 2.

As in D 1 but now the middle player can attempt to intercept the ball as it is chipped over him.

In 4's, 3 v 1. In an area 40 yds x 20 yds or 30 x 30. A, B and C inter-pass against D, an opponent. Diagram 7. A, B and C are never allowed to stand behind D to wait for passes but they move behind him to receive them. 'Ordinary' passes between A, B and C score no points but any pass over D to a player moving there to collect a pass scores one.

Any player considering a chipped pass over D must hide his intentions until he sees the space clear and a receiver showing his intention to move there after the pass has been signaled. When A, B or C receive the ball they must release it with a second touch.

(c) Development 3. (Diagram 8)

12 players, 3 v 2 in each of two zones. The practice area is 80 yards long and 40 yards wide.

D, E and F in the mid-zone inter-pass to set up passes for A, B and F behind them so that A, B or F can deliver passes over the mid-zone into the forward end zone.

All five mid-zone players may follow the ball D, E and F trying to score, Y and Z defending. End zone players A, B, and F together with W, X move forward into the mid-zone. When an attack ends, practice is repeated in the opposite direction. The F players are always on the side which is attacking.

  • A goal scored gains three points, a shot on target one point,
  • A pass which runs out of play in an end zone loses two points.
  • A pass failing to clear the mid-zone loses the passing team one point.

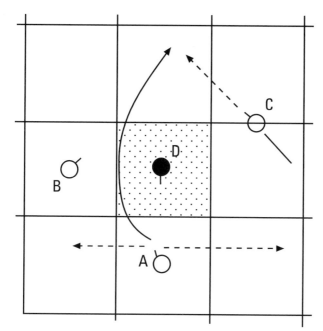

Diagram 7. *Chipping passes over a mid-zone interception and into space.*

Play moves back and forward as defenders turn into attackers and so on.

The mid zone may be made larger or smaller according to the 'chipping' skills of the players.

(d) End Activity.

In conclusion and in pairs, A makes a ground pass to B from about ten yards. Having made the pass A turns and moves away from B. B tries to chip the ball over A's head or shoulder for him to run onto.

Preparation enables a teacher to follow a reasonable plan by organizing his work to optimize effectiveness. Players know that their teacher knows what he is trying to achieve and what their contribution to progress will be. Nevertheless, preparation should never become an end in itself. Talented teachers are opportunists; they sense possibilities, when they occur, for accelerating progress outside what has been prepared for any particular lesson. Opportunities must be taken. Occasionally a whole unit of planning may be revised in order to ride a particular wave of opportunity.

Revision doesn't mean pursuing the players' development 'off the cuff'. It means that a scheduled unit of work or a lesson will be replaced in the order of things elsewhere, certainly not discarded. Prepared work is only discarded when it is clearly failing: it does happen, even for the best teachers, from time to time. True professionals cut their losses; they never allow their egos to get in the way of effectiveness.

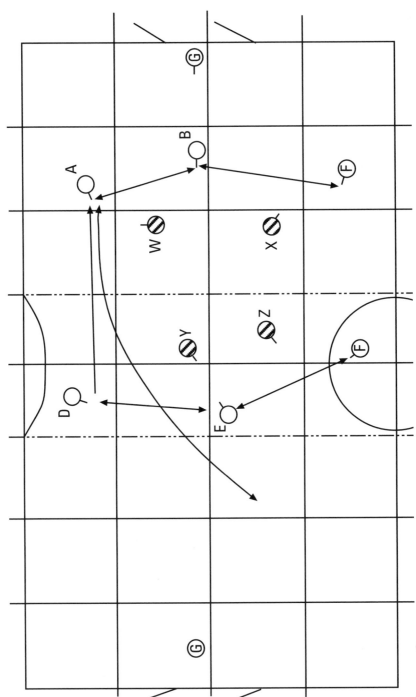

Diagram 8.

3.4 Player Motivation and Management.

Many coaches have made their names and reputations on their powers of motivation. A select number of teachers, in all kinds of human skill and endeavor, become almost revered for their abilities for 'getting the best out of their students'. The implication in both cases is of a power to understand the ways in which the minds of their players work; an insight which seems fundamental to lifting performances to otherwise unattainable heights. Having said that, we appear to know very little about this 'gift' or 'skill'. If it is the former, clearly we can do nothing about it; you either have it or you don't. However, if it is a skill then it can be learned and taught; I am sure that it can.

Certain personality characteristics may be inherited but the majority will have been acquired, albeit at very early ages.

Perhaps a consideration of the psychological factors which we can identify as being connected with soccer performance in practice and in competition will help teachers to understand the mental make-up and the attitudes of players. Improved understanding should enable perceptive teachers to decide which of their players' personality traits will give them the most profitable access to successful motivation.

3.41 Personality Traits.

Some sports psychologists have tried to analyze the mental make up of top players, to identify the different characteristics which seem to make up the successful 'athletic sports' personality. The following are some of their findings.

(a) Drive - an inner capacity by which a player has to seek success in a chosen human activity; he or she are said to be 'driven' by the urge to succeed, implying that the drive is something over which he can exert little if any control. A 'driven' player enjoys the objectivity of sport and winning is everything. He is motivated by clear goals through the achievement of which he can measure his performance in practice or in competition: especially in competition.

(b) Aggression - the capacity for attacking and thereby eliminating any problem which stands in the way of success. An aggressive player is prone to anger, especially if confronted by a problem, e.g. another player, with which or with whom he has difficulty in coping.

Nevertheless, controlled and channeled aggression can be an important factor in successful soccer performance.

Aggressive players should receive recognition and reward for controlling their aggression and by winning as a result of that control.

Aggressive players usually respond well to being teamed up with similar players in practice.

(c) Determination - the ability to sustain whatever action is necessary to reach a desired level of success and a refusal to be deflected from that end. These are the players who, in match play, have never lost until they have left the field of play or until the 'fat lady' is in full song. Players high in determination will respond to open acknowledgment of their 'persistence' but occasionally it may be applied in unprofitable, even undesirable activity. With highly determined players there is always the possibility that they may be determined to have their own way, disregarding team achievement. A sensible teacher will reward determination used to overcome obstacles to more skillful performance in practice or in play.

(d) Leadership - the characteristic shown in a player's willingness to stand up and be counted, especially when the outcome of an issue may show him in a good or a not so good light. Players must be taught to accept responsibility for their own actions whatever the consequences; a leader will be the first to accept those consequences. Some players are 'up front' leaders; they want to be seen to be at the front. Others are more aware of the need for group agreement in certain soccer situations and prefer to lead from 'within'. They are more concerned with the effect and value of any decision or action taken and its beneficial effects on team performance than with individual glory.

There are those who want to be leaders and those we need to be leaders; they are not always the same people.

(e) Self Confidence - players with high self confidence are very sure of themselves. New situations, likely to cause trepidation, even panic, among those less confident, are enjoyed by these players. The more demanding the conditions the greater the degree of assurance and such players can transmit their confidence to those around them. Self confidence should not be confused with arrogance or extravagant exhibitions of assurance; both might well be signs of inferiority complexes rather than the genuine condition. Quiet, even confidential acknowledgment of their superiority in this characteristic is all that these fortunate players need. Other players are only too aware of it.

(f) Emotional Control - often associated with self confidence. Players high in control, in this sense, are not 'fazed' by stress and are slow to demonstrate feelings of anxiety. They recover quickly from what to other players may be traumatic incidents: a first goal scored by opponents in the final fifteen minutes of an important match for example.

A key player 'sent off' or injured or an 'own goal' scored in the most unlucky circumstances are also examples of trauma. Other players need to understand how reassurance, frequently and confidently administered, will help emotional stress to be stabilized. These players need to know, often, how important their stability is to team efforts. The more confident the other players are that a player will 'stay cool' the more he is likely to do so.

(g) Mental Toughness - contains elements of determination, drive and aggression. This player can stand criticism; he may even revel in it. Personal failure can hurt some players but this player is untouched by it: at least it seems as though he is.

'When the going gets tough, the tough get going'.

These are the psychological 'hard men' in sport. Some players relish the physical confrontation, player against player, the genuinely mentally tough enjoy all confrontation but they are unlikely to show it by as much as a flicker of an eye lash. These players relish demands made upon them: the greater the demand the better. They don't need obvious recognition frequently administered. The occasional 'salute' is all that's necessary, they know where they stand in the order of battle. . . at the front!

(h) Coachability - there are players who want to know and learn every- thing; there are those who are almost unteachable: both may be very good players. A highly coachable player may hold the teacher or coach and the coaching process in too high regard. His respect for HOW he has been taught may blunt his ability to assess the value of WHAT he has been taught. To that extent he may be too coach dependent. Some highly coachable players pose great problems: excessive coach dependence inhibits individual initiative and yet these players, above all others, appeal to the teacher's ego: dangerous things, egos!

(i) Conscientiousness - take the trouble to explain to these players their precise place in the scheme of things and they will apply themselves total- ly. They will 'see' quicker than most how group, team and teacher com- mitment to a common cause is the best way forward. Highly conscien- tious players are easily let down because their personal standards are so high. It must be explained to them that while others in the group may not be able to attain their high standards in conscientiousness they will have other qualities which can be deployed to everyone's advantage.

Excessive conscientiousness may be resented by some group members and those practicing it may become the subject of ridicule unless the teacher's antennae are in good working order.

(j) Trust - players must learn to trust each other and the teacher or coach in team games.

For example, a young player who consistently moves into good positions to receive the ball from a particular teammate but never gets it is likely to lose his trust not only in that teammate but in other players as well. The teacher must insert himself between two potentially conflicting interests and set himself up to be trusted by both. He has to educate both players and others to understand what might happen from all points of view in the group's interest.

Some players are very trusting and can as a consequence be severely hurt by any abuse of that trust. Mutual trust is a fundamental requirement in competitive soccer and in the learning and teaching process. Many top coaches develop 'us against them' attitudes among their players.

Carried to excess, though, that attitude seals a group off from anyone seeking or needing to join it, a condition which is a barrier to changes in team personnel and thereby, sooner or later to improvement.

3.42 Motivation.

We have examined some of the characteristics of motivation; there will be others, depending on how individual teachers and coaches 'see' the process. We use different words to describe these characteristics but words often have slightly different meanings for the people using them. To motivate players we need to understand why players do or don't do certain things. Teaching must involve improvement through change.

Understanding why players have different attitudes to what they do and thereby to change itself, is the key to teaching success.

Dangerous statements are often made by people who should but don't know better. Statements such as, 'some players are 'naturals' or 'he was born to be a soccer player' or 'he has ability which you can't teach'. The implication is that however hard others practice and irrespective of how well they are taught or coached, they can never reach the level of the so-called 'naturals'.

There is no such thing as a natural soccer player; soccer players aren't born they are made, even if sometimes they make themselves.

Some may have anatomical advantages or disadvantages, height and build for example, but players of vastly different builds and heights have become world class. Some players may seem to possess certain inherited neuro-physiological advantages, speed of reaction for example, but there have been truly great players whose speed of anticipation has more than compensated for lack of reaction speed or even speed of movement.

Most youngsters given the right attitude to practice and play. . . and to teaching. . . can become better than average soccer players, some of them outstandingly better. It is all in the mind.

3.43 Human Needs.

A number of psychologists have suggested that all human beings, from birth or even before it, have certain needs which they are driven to satisfy, to a greater or lesser extent. As we pass through various levels of individual and social development those needs change, but we never totally release the lower needs with which we were born and brought up in early life.

In diagram 9, the lowest level of needs are those connected with basic survival: air to breathe, food to eat, liquid to drink, sleep to recover, light, warmth and so on. Deprivation of these needs and the sense of threat and deep discomfort with which it is associated stay with us forever. However, as we learn how to satisfy those needs, largely independent of others, they lose some of their importance, but never entirely.

Diagram 9. The Hierarchy of Human Needs.

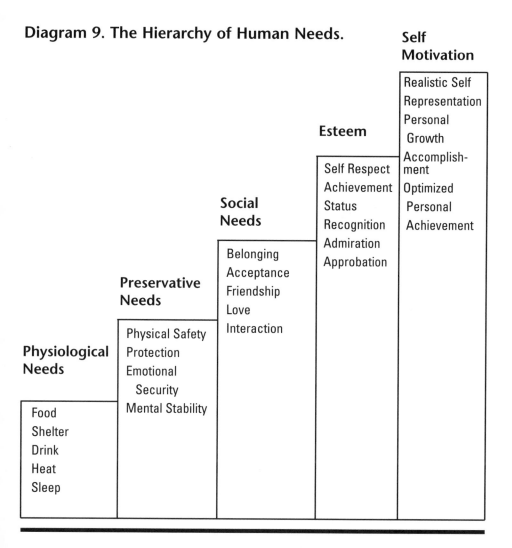

As we grow and become less dependent on bodily needs and more confident of their accessibility, we have a need to feel sure of where we are and what we are doing; we need to feel secure and protected in what may still seem a threatening environment.

A third level of needs is associated with moving out and away from family protection and control to develop wider, social connections: going to school, forming friendship groups, joining play groups, clubs, gangs and soccer teams. We develop a need to belong: some are driven to satisfy these needs powerfully, others less so.

As we develop further many of us, seeking greater independence, are driven towards greater self respect together with the status and recognition which we feel goes with it. We involve ourselves in and become significant contributors to those social groups in which needs for self esteem, personal pride and similar drives can be satisfied.

Basic needs are now less important, almost forgotten by some, less so by others but never forgotten altogether.

Finally at what might be described, perhaps wrongly, as the highest level of aspiration, we seek. . . or some do. . . greater self-realization; we are less driven by how others see us than by how we see ourselves. Our accomplishments are subject to self-evaluation; we are capable of assessing our value to ourselves critically, without ulterior motives almost: 'almost' because we are never totally free from what we were or from those early, basic drives.

There are important implications for soccer teachers and especially for coaches if they fail to take players' basic needs into account. Dropping a player from a team, even moving him from a group of his choice to another, may represent a serious threat to his sense of security. If so, the teacher should expect resentment and resistance.

We all tend to withdraw into a secure level of need satisfaction when a higher need is threatened.

As we satisfy one level of need we become aware, instinctively, of other needs growing within us which begin to demand satisfaction.

Changing needs are the keys to motivation, it is important to understand how they work; they cannot be ignored. Drives are the foundations upon which intelligent soccer teachers create their motivational systems of incentives and rewards; they will need them!

3.42 Incentives and Rewards.
Incentives are what we are promised before and if we achieve certain levels of performance or behavior; rewards are what we actually get. They are not the same and are frequently misused by teachers, managers and coaches in sport, especially where the latter doesn't match up with the former.

Only make promises which you can definitely keep.

Incentives are promissory attempts to affect performance before it actually takes place. They are assumed to affect attitudes: to improve a player's motivation by appealing to his needs. They may do so but often in ways not foreseen by those using them. Incentives are commonly assumed to be 'material' in soccer; this is not necessarily so. Many people in sport, especially in professional sport, assume that all players are motivated by materialistic rewards: all may appear to be but appearances can be deceptive.

To mature sportsmen and women, materialistic motivational attempts may be insulting. They are likely to react accordingly with cynical disregard for those making the offers.

Promissory incentives can provoke undesirable, unforeseen attitudes towards desirable achievement. In practice groups, where players are promoted or relegated on the basis of practice performances, the prospect of promotion may be a complete 'turn off' to the less skillful who quickly work out (or assume) that they will never be skillful enough to gain promotion. Clever teachers devise tests of progress and ability which allow everyone to earn something in the way of recognition even if it's group applause.

In professional leagues, lasting many months, it is very difficult for a coach to maintain enthusiasm for practice or even for playing when players know or assume that they have no chance of winning the competition. At the beginning of a competitive season, teams should be given markers towards rewards for agreed levels of achievement other than winning a certain competition.

There's not much incentive or reward in a situation where one team or player wins and everyone else is a loser.

Inflated incentives can affect player performance excessively because their effect is difficult to control by the teacher or coach. Rewards on the other hand, administered shrewdly, can have highly beneficial effects, especially when they are given unexpectedly. They are even more effective when they are exclusive.

On English coaching courses, highly priced, international players competed in 'recreational' six-a-side games with almost demonic commitment and total disregard for personal safety. The desperately sought prizes on offer were two dollar tie clips. The clips carried the crest of the England Football Association and were to that extent exclusive. Their intrinsic value was almost nil: their extrinsic value was beyond price, especially since everyone knew that the clips could not be bought at any price.

A famous German national coach, when I asked what he would like in recognition of his contribution to an international coaching seminar replied, instantly, "Your tracksuit top!"

Less than a dozen coaches in England were entitled to wear those particular garments.

The same track suit tops could also be an embarrassment. They were worn only by the permanent national coaches. To some coaches outside that select group they became a source of jealousy; they signified an almost unattainable level of status in the national coaching structure. 'Wear them but don't flaunt them', was my only solution.

Incentives and rewards as motivational devices merit a lot of careful thought. Get it right and a teacher is riding high; get it wrong and all manner of problems, many unsolvable, occur.

We are all children at heart and recognition, in some form or other, is what we search for all our lives.

3.5 Managing Players.
The management of young players is a matter of:
    (a) finding out what their expectations of the teaching situation are.
    (b) assessing the realism of their expectations.
    (c) consulting them with a view to arriving at realistic objectives.
    (d) seeking and agreeing the measures by which achievement will be measured and reviewed.
    (e) exercising power and authority with sensitivity, sympathy and above all with fairness.

Managing young players, or not so young players, is much like managing people in any walk of life in which productivity is the aim. Players need to know what's in it for them: what is in store for them: what they will be expected to contribute: how they will progress and to what extent the whole business will be interesting, enjoyable and rewarding.

There also needs to be discussion and agreement about what the teacher seeks to get out of the action and what he expects the players to put in. If his needs are incompatible with theirs, trouble and tension are inevitable: better solve those problems at day one rather than later.

'Put out the fires before they start', as my Irish grandmother would say.

Too many people seek and take up leadership, teaching or coaching positions with young players in the expectation that all contributions will be gratefully received, by the players that is.

Even less admirably, they impose relationships which allow them to massage their own egos while doing precious little for the egos and aspirations of the players.

Young players need firm, demanding and scrupulously fair leadership . . . from the front: most want it.

That flies in the face of some exotic education philosophies in recent years. A belief that all teaching should be centered exclusively on the wants and the needs of children, in that order, has been widespread. Many teachers have been persuaded that young players can somehow discover everything for themselves given reasonable time and latitude: soccer teachers have neither!

Others have been convinced (or have convinced themselves) that young players should do what they want to do whenever they want to do it, in other words that they should manage themselves. Inevitably the players finish up managing their teachers.

Soccer teachers have limited time and opportunities at their disposal. Most young players are in a desperate hurry to be as skillful (clever) as possible as soon as possible: so both teachers and players are in a hurry. Speed of achievement (and satisfaction) will only come from organization; organization must be founded upon some clear acknowledgments.

(a) While discussion may be profitable, ultimately the teacher decides what should happen; that's why he is the teacher.

(b) The teacher's superior experience of teaching and of the game qualifies him to be the one to whom the others listen. After the players listen to him, he listens to them but in that order.

(c) Teaching and learning cannot proceed without order: those intent upon disorder should be advised to find another team, better still another game.

(d) A teacher has the responsibility for setting the standards by which the quality of action is measured. Without standards in teaching, in performance and in personal presentation the whole business is seriously devalued.

(e) Standards are as much concerned with the ethics of general social conduct and behavior as with behavior in match play and in practice. Soccer players should understand that they represent their teacher, the game and everyone connected with it, wherever they are and whatever they do.
The higher the level of involvement the more that is true but, unfortunately, the less it is accepted.
Sport (soccer) is either an activity in which people can learn and demonstrate civilized behavior towards each other or it's not worth our time.

(f) Teaching and learning are best achieved on the basis of mutual respect: it has to be earned. Nevertheless the teacher is responsible for order and for discipline and he cannot delegate that responsibility.

(g) The ultimate criterion of successful management must be the extent to which players become capable of managing themselves.

3.6 Communication.

Teachers, by definition, are communicators: they show and demonstrate: they speak and tell: they touch and manipulate: they listen and hear. . . or they should!

Communication in teaching has to be a multi-directional process. A teacher needs to know how effective in communication he has been and can only know if those being taught communicate back to him: give him 'feed-back' as it is called.

Soccer teachers most commonly use a combination of visual, verbal and auditory communication. They show players what to do and how to do it; they comment on how things are done or should be done; they listen to hear what players say while trying to use soccer skills; they touch players to emphasize a point, to establish persuasive contact or to place a limb in a better functional position, when kicking the ball to achieve certain flight effects for example.

3.61 Demonstration.

Sports teaching and coaching places great importance on showing players and athletes 'how'. Seeing what is done and how to do it is a highly effective teaching and inspirational process but only if players:
- know what they should be looking for and at.
- can see what is important from the same viewpoint as the teacher.
- appreciate fully what the purpose of the demonstration is.
- feel that acquiring skills is easier, from what has been shown.

For example, observing a player 'chipping' a ball from a position on the same side as the kicking foot, from behind the kicking foot or from the front or 'ball side' of the kicking foot may produce quite different visual impressions of how best to execute the technique. If the teacher comments on what is happening from a different position entirely, it is probable that attention to key technical points will be misdirected and ineffective.

What players are placed to look at may not be what they need to see!

We all learn by similar processes but with different emphases and at different speeds. Some players respond best to a 'watch and try' exposure. Others need key factors to be identified for them before they actually experience the skill. Teachers can be too technical.

Soccer teaching is best directed by what players need to know and what information they can handle. Too much technical input produces information indigestion.

It seems obvious, but often isn't, that a teacher without the ability to demonstrate well, shouldn't! Soccer teaching has gained enormously from the miles of tv, video and film footage and the ready accessibility of recorders and play back apparatus. The very best players in the world can be seen in play and in practice for as long as players or teachers want to watch them. The teacher's function is to direct players' attention to the performance points which matter.

Professional soccer is a great 'show' and many of its players are show-men; they often elaborate their skills for show rather than for effect. Nothing wrong in that as long as other players don't pursue the spectac-ular while ignoring the substance. A teacher must sort out the key points in performance without which young players may learn more of how not to play rather than how.

Without film or video a teacher may use the demonstrational ability of his outstanding players and will do so even if he himself was or is a skillful player. Recognition (reward), as we saw earlier, comes in different forms and young players chosen to demonstrate will see that as recognition and reward.

3.62 Verbalizing.

The use of words can be a tricky business, made trickier by teachers who assume that they speak the same language as their players; many don't and don't know that they don't!

Soccer coaches and teachers have benefited from enormous advances in sports technology in recent times but one disadvantage has been the tendency for both to use 'buzz words', words which are designed to veil their work in mystique. Their use may or may not indicate superior levels of soccer expertise at a teacher's command but they are likely to mean nothing to most players, especially to young players.

And young players themselves, in their own private worlds, develop special words and phrases used to establish separate identities from most adults. We all like to feel that we are 'special', hence our use of distinctive, exclusive and often colorful language.

Teachers are well advised to learn the language of those with whom they expect to communicate. If they cannot, the effectiveness of their teaching depends on frequent checks to ensure that what they have said has been clearly understood. Most young players, even the not so young, are unlikely to admit that they haven't understood if that could be seen as a confession of limited intelligence.

'Think what you need to say. . . really need to say. . . and precisely how you are going to say it', is sound advice for everyone in the communica-tion business.

If you haven't anything constructive and important to say, say nothing. Good teachers know what to say, when to say it and when to keep quiet.

3.63 Experiential Learning.

Many of the world's best players were, to certain levels of performance, self taught. They were exceptionally highly motivated towards soccer skill and made extraordinary commitments to practice and play from very early ages. They developed technical trickery and confidence rarely if ever possible through formalized teaching alone. Very few youngsters today would be allowed to practice for six, seven or more hours each day. Even so, a soccer teacher must try to short circuit this vast, experiential learning commitment by creating trial and success rather than the trial and error situations which unstructured learning often becomes.

A soccer teacher must understand the game well enough to be able to see how the 'pieces' of soccer fit into the whole jig-saw.

For example, it is one thing to know and show a player how to strike the ball when shooting in practice but match play goal scoring requires a player to:

(a) Have good striking techniques,
(b) Sense (or know) what a goalkeeper is likely to do when faced with different shooting possibilities,
(c) Be able to change technique, body position and speed and still score,
(d) 'Read' what alternative options are created by the presence of other attackers and defenders and know how to use or pretend to use those options.
(e) Put failure behind him but learn from experience immediately.

Effective teaching only occurs when a teacher can create realistic practice situations within which a player is more successful than not but which expose his developing skills to subtle tests and trials.

Soccer skills are as much a matter of what goes on between a player's ears as outside them: at the highest levels of play even more so.

Finally, communication is a two way process; it involves hearing, seeing, feeling, thinking and responding by both parties! A teacher who, over-anxious to get on with what he sees as a player's needs, fails to hear what the player says or see what he does is coaching soccer, not a soccer player.

Teaching from the front is desirable and often necessary but it pays to look behind occasionally in case no one is there!

Chapter 4
Acquiring Soccer Skill

4.1 What Is Soccer Skill?

Before deciding how best to acquire and develop soccer skill it is necessary to clear up a great deal of confusion about what it is.

Soccer skill is learned action, formed out of a variety of minor specific actions, which can be produced and reproduced on demand when playing the game, with other players and against other players.

It involves the capacities of one group of players to maneuver and manipulate a ball between them, or individually, to score goals and thereby to defeat an opposing and usually equal group of players trying to prevent them from so doing.

The 'variety of minor actions' referred to and used in playing the game, hereafter called technical skills (techniques) and tactical skills, are legal or illegal as prescribed in the laws of the game.

Teachers must fully understand the need to relate all that they do for and with young players to 'in the game' performance of some kind. The prospect of producing players capable of sustained and entertaining ball juggling, using unlikely parts of their anatomies, may be attractive to some teachers and many parents but it has nothing whatever to do with developing soccer skill. In the context of the soccer game, it is a waste of practice time other than for whatever sensory pleasure it gives.

The use of technical and tactical skills may be subjected to prescribed levels of direct, physical interference.

The game allows for significant athletic and occasionally gymnastic capacities to enhance players' techniques and skills. It also specifically includes the use of bodily contact, the shoulder charge. These considerations are all part of what becomes, ultimately, soccer skill. Teachers and coaches cannot and should not ignore their existence when teaching and coaching. They may be inconvenient but they are part of the game; eventually they must be part of practice.

4.11 What Is A Skillful Soccer Player?

The judgment of a soccer player as skillful or not so skillful may be based on the answers to some or all of the following questions.

It may be useful to place players somewhere along a continuum of 0 to 5 for each consideration.

1. When receiving the ball how close is his control?
2. To what extent does he run the ball confidently and deceptively or uncertainly and obviously?

3. How accurate is he when striking the ball, long or short.
4. Can he make space, and therefore time, for himself when under pressure from opponents?
5. Are his individual skills 'sure' enough to get him out of difficulties during a game?
6. To what degree does he play for himself or for others (the team)? Can he do both if required?
7. Does he pose difficult problems for opponents with and without the ball or is he easily 'read'?
8. Can he free himself from a tight marking opponent and can he free teammates if need be?
9. Does he only react to what has happened or is he a move or two ahead of it?
10. Is he a far sighted player or can he only see what is happening close to himself and the ball?
11. Has he good or poor athletic ability and does he use what he has sensibly?

These factors may be 'weighted' according to the maturity of the player and more factors may be added as a young player moves into high class soccer, but for teachers these will do.

All the factors will receive attention from a soccer teacher during the development process. The extent to which one factor, or circumstances arising out of it, receive special and more detailed attention during directed practice will depend upon the players' levels of need.

Skill is often judged by the ease with which a player accomplishes something in the game. A skillful player's movements are assured and economically smooth: the certainty of his movements with or without the ball are unaffected by any demands for extra speed or accuracy. It is important that players are given this information and that they are party to agreement about practice objectives and how they are to be achieved.

4.12 What Is A Skillful Game Of Soccer.

Skillful players should produce skillful soccer but unless they have clear ideas how the game is judged, they may experience difficulties. Ten individualists exhibiting their personal skills for the sake of exhibition can produce games which are as boring as ten players abusing the ball by kicking it aimlessly and hopelessly.

The following should find widespread agreement.

During a skillful game of soccer:

(a) The ball is mostly on the ground.
(b) The ball is passed around accurately and deceptively.
(c) Shots at goal occur frequently and accurately.

(d) Shooting chances are created with high perception and purpose-
     fully.
(e) Passing moves are varied with individual cleverness and dribbling.
(f) Players have space in which to play.
(g) Play has a clear pattern and purpose.
(h) There are frequent positional interchanges.
(i) Attackers can exploit their skills and are not subjected to intimida-
     tion or to foul play.
(j) Defending players mark, cover, intercept and tackle skillfully
     and fairly.
(k) Goalkeepers are not merely shot stoppers they are integral parts of
     defense and attack. Increasingly, they require secure 'outfield'
     techniques: controlling, with all parts of the body: long and short
     passing, even heading on occasions.

These factors will be major points of reference when teaching and
developing skillful individual soccer players into successful team players.

4.2 The Learning Process.
4.21 Percepts, Precepts and Concepts.
Traditionally, educational and training processes start with the simple and
move on to the complex as human capacities expand and consolidate
learned experience. In soccer teaching and coaching it may better serve
our purpose to begin with a detailed consideration of the whole skill with
which we are involved. If we start at the top, teachers who are concerned
with player development at early stages will be able to see, much more
clearly, how their contribution fits in to the 'whole' picture of soccer skill.
The whole skill for those working with very young players need not be full
11 v 11 soccer but it will involve one 'group' playing against another,
three a side, six against six, even four versus three, might be the full game
for beginners and young players. Indeed small games feature prominently in the daily training and practice of senior professionals in England
although I'm not certain that their coaches know why, other than when
they also want a game!

As an example let us examine the full picture in which a striker uses his
skills in creating shooting chances and other options in or near to the
penalty area.

Often under severe pressure, he must pass, dribble, turn and shoot, or
'fake' (pretend) any of those options, with the most acute awareness of
space and the actions of all the players in it: his own and opponents.
These involve highly sophisticated, tactical skill, positional awareness and
technical touch and could involve all or some of the following:
(a) Receiving passes played through narrow gaps between the front
     curtain of defenders. Diagram 10.

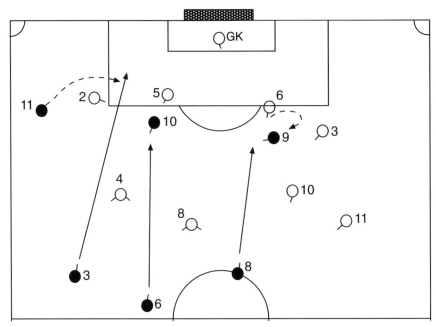

Diagram 10. *Passing through gaps in the front defensive curtain.*

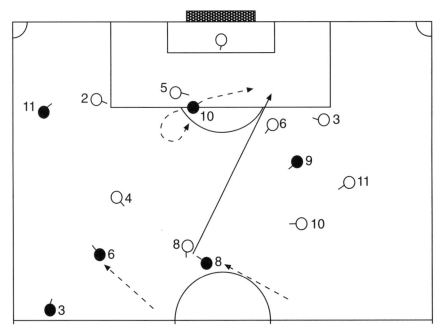

Diagram 11. *Reversing a pass through a gap in the front defensive curtain.*

Passes should be delivered deceptively, with no obvious intention and with optimum control of 'weight'; often they aren't and the receiver has to do what he can with what he gets!

48

(b) Deception achieved by reversing passes to, or into space for, strikers. 'Front' players must understand what the 'feeding' player is trying to acheive and adjust their positions accordingly. Diagram 11.

(c) The 'feeding' player following his pass in while looking for a shooting set-up for himself first touch or for other players on second touch.

(d) Receiving passes 'on the bounce' or on the ground, and 'laying off' passes in all directions with the inside of the foot, the outside of the foot, with flicks and back heels, accurately and with good sense, i.e. perceptively.

(e) 'Fake' moves by potential receivers to gain starting advantages over markers; these moves must be taught, practiced and timed precisely.

(f) Passes 'faked' to create space and time for a shot on the turn.

(g) Feeders and receivers of passes predicting the reaction moves of opposing defenders.

(h) Combined moves between attackers precisely integrated through a highly developed awareness of opportunity and capability.

(i) The need for instant and acute perception of space: how to create it: how to hold it: how, where and when to move it and so on.

These nine technical and tactical objectives make up most of the whole picture. With professionals, teaching might begin at any stage according to the players' abilities and awareness of need. The first phase in the process for mature, well educated players might be to present the whole picture. All the defending players and all the opposing attack plus a full complement of support players.

The coach sets out and seeks agreement on practice objectives and watches practice develop until the opportunity arises to identify and emphasize a major objective within the 'big picture'. This is the basis for the introduction of a relevant practice phase. He then dissembles the big picture and works with key players on important constituent parts.

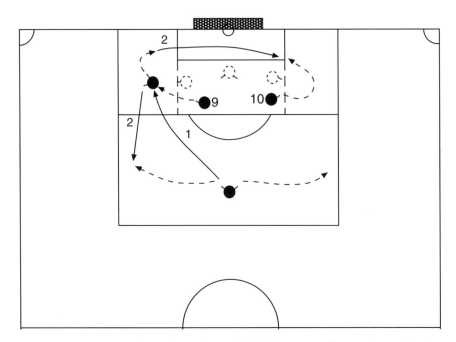

Diagram 12. *Area 40 yards X 40 yards. Technical (perceptual) practice to develop the skill of moving to receive passes in wide positions and subsequently to select and practice the various technical options available.*

4.211 Perceptual Learning.

Even for professionals this may mean taking practice down to quite elementary, unopposed, technical (perceptual) levels.

Here two strikers are working on receiving passes following the wide (split) runs needed to draw central markers away from each other and away from a probable free back behind them. The 'ghost' defenders shown are not available in the early stages of practice but may be introduced as the attacking group becomes more skillful at defeating the limited opposition.

Even professional players may have one 'good' foot with the other an embarrassment. 'One footedness' is a severe but common handicap to the development of tactical competence. It often necessitates taking a player back to the most elementary stages of skill learning to rehabilitate him.

Mature players should of course have a learning speed superior to that of very young players, nevertheless the process will be much the same.

In diagram 13, players are using 'round' practices to enable them to learn (to be taught) how to use their weaker feet more effectively in function related technique practices. Opposition is introduced gradually and when players' skill development and practice success warrants it. 'Round' practices enable a practice sequence to move from one 'end' of a group to the other continuously.

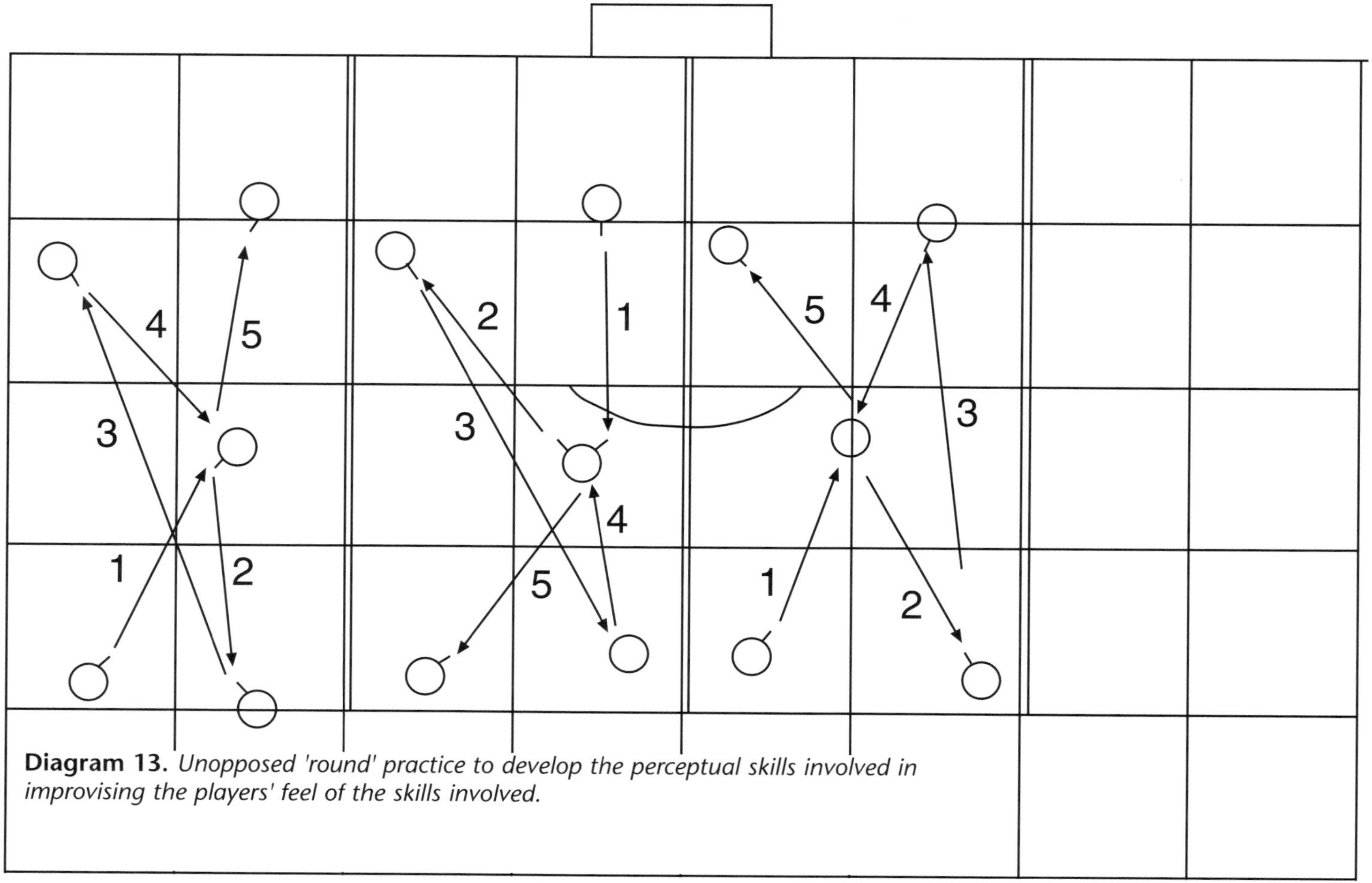

Diagram 13. *Unopposed 'round' practice to develop the perceptual skills involved in improvising the players' feel of the skills involved.*

In diagram 14, the practice aim is to improve ground passing through defensive gaps; receiving players practice controlling, turning and passing. There is no opposition initially but players should be encouraged to imagine the counter moves of opponents.

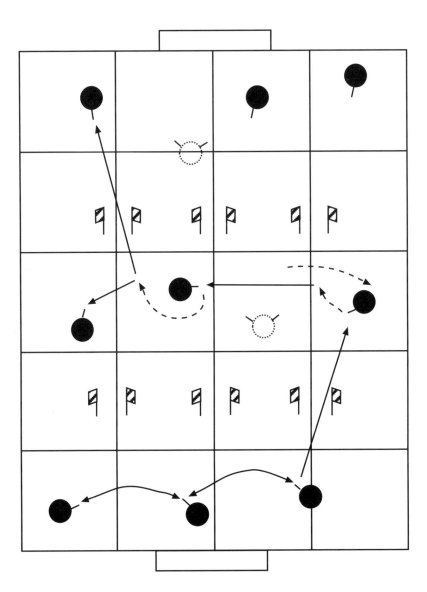

Diagram 14. *Interpassing through gaps between defenders. Technical practice. A later phase involves the introduction of one and eventually two opponents in each zone.*

Vivid imagination, as I said earlier is a very important ability, especially where players practice alone against a rebound surface.

The gaps will vary in width according to players' skill levels.

Later an opponent may patrol the mid zone to test the players' ability to react to changed options.

The objective of the practice is to improve and consolidate new technical competence and to prepare for its transfer into match performance.

In diagram 14, the players in the end zones may begin in 2 v 1 or 3 v 1 situations moving up to 3 v 2 and 4 v 2 according to improvement.

Finally goals are introduced along the end lines so that, having received passes through gaps, the receiving three (or four) can inter-pass to shoot and score.

In diagram 15, in what are virtually two penalty areas (overall area is 40 yds x 40), all players must remain in their own zones. A, B, C and, if necessary, D inter-pass to find gaps between or outside the two black defenders in front of them. Strikers E and F are opposed by one defender and the goalkeeper. As the two strikers control and turning skills improve they could be limited to playing in the two central squares only. Alternatively another defender and another striker could be added to advance the problems and to further test their new skills.

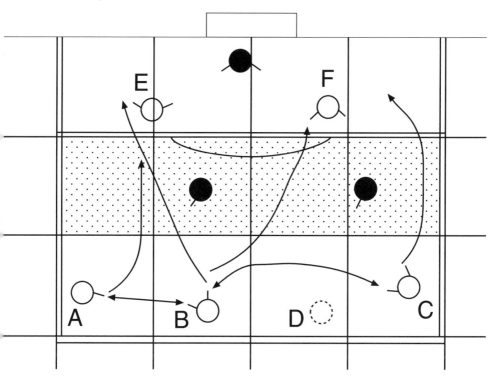

Diagram 15. *Passing through gaps for strikers on goal.*

Players' willingness to 'imagine' realism into practices in many ways dictates the extent to which they can or will practice effectively.

Practice begins with an overall assessment of the problems posed. We break down the overall problem into practice parts at levels determined by the players' abilities. Initially these may be isolated, unopposed technical repetitions with minimal and restricted opposition included when appropriate.

As improvement occurs so increased degrees of difficulty are introduced, one or more opponents and one or more co-operating players. Gradually the practice is being reconstituted towards the original 'big picture'.

Perceptual practices occur at the earliest stage in learning when players suffer no interference in what are technical exercises, sometimes called drills.

With modifications of distances between practicing groups, the practice set ups will be just as suitable for young players as for professionals.

All young players up to the age of ten years or thereabouts should be heavily involved in this type of practice. Game awareness (sense) will not be taught as such, unless exceptional opportunities occur. Should it manifest itself, it will of course receive approval. Young players acquire an increasing 'game awareness' by playing a great deal of casual mini soccer, 1 v 1, 3 v 3 up to 6 v 6 for ten year olds, and 'conditioned' variations of it.

4.212 Preceptual Learning.

I shall take as an example the working relationship between the two strikers: where to move and why: when to move: how to move and so on. This involves fundamental soccer principles or precepts. The same precepts, in my view, are valid for any free moving, dribbling, passing and 'shooting' (scoring) game such as field hockey, basketball, rugby, football and the like.

Practice, almost always, will have some degree of opposition even though, in the early stage of practice development, the opposing player or players will be strictly controlled by the teacher.

'Shadow practice', about which I have more to say elsewhere, doesn't need opposing players other than in the imaginations of those taking part.

In this phase, the strikers will receive passes and fake a turn in one direction but spin away to shoot from the other. Their main option will be to reverse those options, to fake a shot, turn and pass (or shoot) moving the 'other way'. Initially the strikers practice the moves and options perceptually and away from the players who will provide opposition later. Teaching tactical moves successfully, involving precepts as most do, may be confidential initially: and it has to be successful!

The precepts involved here might be:

(1) The quicker a player is the quicker the reactions which he provokes. This is particularly relevant to strikers.

(2) When the ball is being moved towards goal, space is likely to be found most easily behind it.

(3) The penalty area is the safest part of the field. . . for strikers. Having worked their way into the penalty area, it will pay strikers to seek and hold positions between their markers and the lines of possible passes.

(4) Where one striker moves towards a possible pass, the other should move in the opposite direction.

Practice will aim to reinforce and illustrate those precepts and produce situations which the players may explore, taking into account their own strengths and weaknesses with the proviso that the latter will be noted and steps taken to remedy them long or medium term.

Strikers will be taught how to move away from the central striking area so as to move back into it late and decisively. When an opponent is introduced he will be allowed to react to attackers' moves but not to play the ball.

Players upon whom practice is focused must always have a significant practice advantage.

In the next phase of practice, one defender faces a 2 v 1 situation in a limited area, diagram 16, which he opposes as best he can to prevent the strikers from scoring. The strikers look to use the skills and principles explored in previous practices. Depending on the strikers' response success, the practice may be raised to a 2 v 2 situation and then to 2 v 3 as progress occurs.

No one can lay down fixed lines or rates of progression. The players make those decisions by the rate at which they show improvement in performance or in understanding.

Where there are now two central backs opposing the two advanced strikers, the strikers are taught how to stretch the two defenders and how to gain a start advantage in moving away from an opponent to get in a shot or pass. This involves learning how to make space. They will be taught how to stretch (pull apart) two or more opponents: how to gain a start advantage in racing an opponent for the ball. These objectives involve basic precepts, or action rules if you like, which are always valid.

Deception of course is a fundamental precept of attacking play.

A few players as young as ten or eleven years may be capable of understanding some of the game's precepts and of applying them intelligently. One of the soccer teacher's problems is to persuade technically skillful,

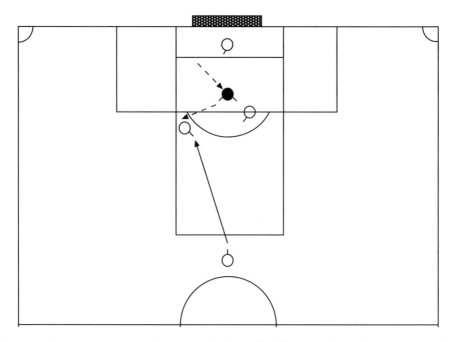

Diagram 16. *Basic preceptual practice for 'twin' strikers involving the principles of where, when and how to move to create shooting chances.*

young players to think about the game, especially those whose technical abilities have been reinforced by outstanding athletic abilities.

'Why exchange certainties for maybes? 'is a difficult question for a teacher to answer. The answer of course lies in the future, but young players are not often interested in the future. It is not easy to convince young, high achievers that some contemporaries are likely to catch up in technique as they grow older and that some may become superior in power which can be used to cancel out technical cleverness. It is difficult for boys who have outstanding technical skill to accept that, one day, technique alone may not be enough.

Talented players often give up when they are caught up.

Teachers must persuade players never to be satisfied with what they are. They must be challenged to extend their horizons: it's not easy, but then who said that teaching is.

Up to about ten years of age, a teacher will concentrate on player perceptions: the seeing, hearing, feeling and above all the 'doing' processes in learning new skills. Young players are naturally selfish; they see soccer situations almost exclusively from their own point of view. However, all practice should end with some form of competitive, small, group play. A perceptive teacher will use game situations or small sided games to introduce and reinforce preceptual ideas even though many players may not fully understand their significance. This constant referral to the game and to game situations is vital to effective learning at all stages.

The game is the 'big jig-saw picture' into which all practice pieces must fit.

Practice games will be biased (conditioned) to ensure optimum success in transferring what has been learned in practice into the game or into a phase of it.

Realistic selection and application of newly acquired techniques and ideas in game situations is crucial to progress.

In diagram 17, (a) the players are repeating, end to end, passing and 'laying off' moves concentrating on technical excellence but judging what to do and when to do it according to the movements of the single opponent at each end of the practice round.

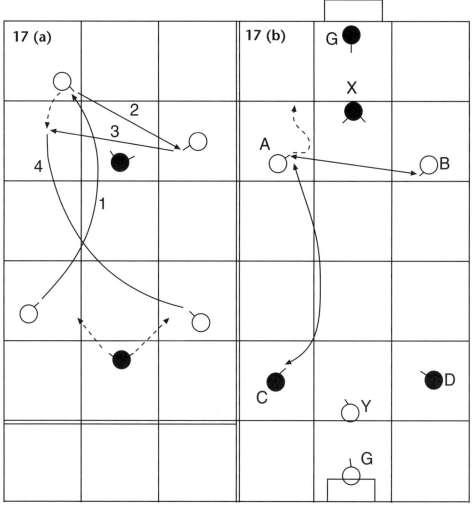

Diagram 17. *(a) and (b). Practice grid end to end passing and laying off.*

The precepts involved here might be:
- (a) Making an obvious move, e.g. a first touch 'lay off', while changing at the last moment to a control and pass move.
- (b) Controlling the ball and playing a pass into space for the second player to move onto and give a first touch pass.
- (c) Controlling the ball with one touch so that a pass can be delivered with the other foot, 'first touch'.
- (d) Receiving the ball by moving towards the pass to control it and passing, or faking to pass, one way but changing to another.
- (e) Controlling the ball and running it at and past the opponent or passing the ball past him.

In diagram 17 (b), the players are using the same basic passing situations but this time practice culminates in shots at goal. The practice area has been lengthened thereby requiring players to pass over the mid zone using different lofted passing techniques. C and D inter-pass against Y to deliver the ball to A or B who inter-pass to shoot. When an attack has finished, A and B become the servers to C and D who try to score at their end of the area.

At the top of the nine to ten years of age band, or thereabouts, most players should be capable of mixing a first choice of action with secondary options. e.g.

- Lay off a pass or 'fake' a lay off but turn and shoot.

- 'Fake' a move in one direction to 'throw' an opponent off balance to gain a start advantage in a different direction.

- Move behind an opponent to get in front of him.

- Accept the close attention of a marker and use your body to 'screen' (hide) the ball as it comes or when you have it.

Opponents, initially, may be directed, even strictly controlled, by the teacher. Controlled opposition in practice is important at all levels of development when new skills are being taught. As players develop a greater awareness of the co-operative possibilities in group interplay, they will be 'worked' using the basic individual principles of play (precepts) as the foundation for problem solving in practice.

These will be dealt with in detail in the final section of this book but here is an example; it involves understanding the importance of certain personal priorities when defending such as:

(1) Preventing opponents from delivering the ball into the penalty area.

(2) Preventing opponents from receiving the ball and turning towards goal to pass, dribble or shoot.
(3) Marking opponents closely enough to allow for reasonable chances of intercepting or tackling for the ball should it come.
(4) Tracking any attacker's forward run towards goal.

Examples of individual precepts in attack are:
(1) Dribbling the ball squarely at a defender to hide any indication of a final move past him.
(2) Taking up 'blind side' positions: keeping a marking opponent between himself and the ball, wherever it is.
(3) Positioning the body between an opponent and the ball (screening) when receiving or holding it.
(4) Moving against the flow of attacking play to set marking problems for opponents.

Some of the 'facts of soccer life' may be learned quite early.
For example:

- without the ability to bring a moving ball under control, a player learns that he can't dribble or shoot or pass.

- without the ability to 'work' the ball with both feet, he learns. . . the hard way. . . that sooner or later opponents will control him because his directional options are limited.

- without the ability to work the ball while 'looking up' and around him, his action horizons will be severely limited.

These are some of the facts of soccer life and are the basis for preceptual learning. Precepts are not commandments, they are not 'musts' but they do offer the highest probabilities for success in play.

4.213 Conceptual Learning.

In diagram 18, two opposing players have been introduced into the practice. The practice space is double an actual penalty area. White A and B inter-pass until they see an opportunity to pass forward to D or C. The receiving player will try to lay off a pass to his partner or back to white A or B, either one of whom (but not both) can follow the pass into the forward area to press home an attack.

The practice aims to create chances for shots at goal. The teacher will introduce action options when possibilities occur. The practice can work end to end as in a small game. Situations arise which require most of the players to judge where they should move, when they should move and

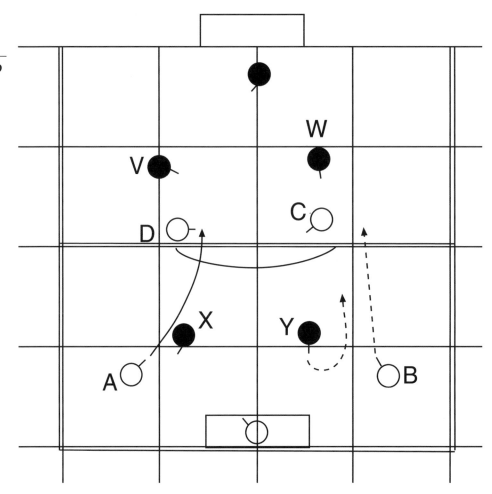

Diagram 18. *Double box practice for one supporting striker.*

how they should move in order to set problems for defenders.

Conceptual learning involves the imaginative development of ideas. The teacher has developed the precepts upon which good attacking play is based a stage further. Now, players must be encouraged to expand their experience and understanding to create their own soccer ideas.

We have moved from learning to 'do' things to applying what can be done in the most reliable ways in game situations. Finally we have learned how to think imaginatively in solving and setting soccer problems.

However high the level to which players aspire, they should never forget the earlier learning stages of repetitive even isolated practice and also the principles of play. Technical skills and principles never become fully automatic, their execution always needs optimum attention.

In the skill development which we have used so far, senior players might move from shadow practice to opposed practice. Here, much younger players look for opportunities to use the techniques and skills learned and practiced as the development of 'free' practice proceeds. Game moves become more important than pure technical exercises. Opposition should provide a controlled, reasonable but never fully inhibiting test of the players' judgments. We are in the try and succeed business, not the try and fail.

The teacher or coach, more likely the latter now, watches for opportunities to make coaching points relating perhaps to where, when and how to make space for shots. This is the conceptual area of learning. To make space in soccer a player needs to understand the roles and responsibilities of opposing players and the precepts (principles) which affect their decisions.

There are irresistible arguments, at all levels of play, for players to be given sustained, serious practice experience in positions opposed to those in which they normally play.

There's no better way to learn to play soccer than by playing it. . . in every position on the pitch.

For example, an attacker will find it useful to know that one of the golden rules for a defender is to position himself between an attacker and the goal and close enough to touch him. The defender should also be in a position, whenever possible, to watch both his opponent and the ball at the same time.

Having gained that insight into defending, an attacker is half way home in devising moves and by taking up positions in which the defender's precepts become difficult if not impossible to apply.

For example, if the attacker 'fakes' a move behind his marker and towards goal, almost certainly the marker will move back towards goal to maintain the positional relationship described earlier. If the attacker quickly moves in front of and away from his marker he is likely to gain a yard or two start advantage. In high class play, 'a yard or two' in the penalty area is as good as a mile!

If the attacker moves back and towards a wider position, his marker will assume that the attacker is trying to move into a 'blind side' position. His reaction is likely to be to move backwards and away from goal with the attacker until the attacker becomes a diminishing threat. i.e. too far from goal and on a very wide (near impossible) shooting angle. Then the marker will stop, track (watch) the attacker's further moves, if any, and reintegrate his own position with those of other defenders. By pulling his marker backwards, the attacker has made space by taking two players out of it: himself and his opponent.

'Collecting defenders and pulling them away from key defensive areas is a highly sophisticated tactical skill: many professional players never learn it because no one has bothered to teach them the principles involved.

This third, conceptual, stage in the teaching and learning process involves players applying their expanding experience and imagination in problem solving. An example of the need for conceptual thinking might be as follows:

Let's assume that orthodox team deployment involves one or two central strikers. If a team lacks players capable of functioning effectively in those roles, it doesn't make much sense to deploy players there merely because everyone else does. There is a powerful inclination in soccer for teams to become dedicated followers of tactical fashion; it should be resisted. In the circumstances, it might pay to play without central attacking players in most phases of play.

Attacking build up might be contrived and sustained away from central areas and only redirected there to suit the capabilities of the players available. All players might be required to stay away from central attacking positions until the very last moment before ball delivery. Central positions leading to strikes on goal might be filled by players moving there from highly unorthodox and thereby surprising parts of the field, very late and very quickly.

It sounds unlikely? Holland could and perhaps should have won the 1974 World Cup using just such methods.

Conceptual practice and teaching is unlikely to be successful much before fourteen years of age, that is to say when the way in which teams develop team strategies and tactics begins to intrigue some of them: the more the better. Problem setting and solving is a valid teaching method for all players, young or mature, so long as the teacher knows most of the answers to the problems he sets. Conceptual thinking is vital to the future of the game and in many ways is the most intriguing part of the whole business of playing, teaching and coaching. While young players are unlikely to be attracted to it much before fourteen years of age they should be exposed to its possibilities.

The following are examples of problem setting and solving:

(a) Two teams are playing 6 v 6 on an area 60 yards x 40 yards. One team is given an extra player.

There are twenty minutes left to play and the score is 1-0 to the team which is one player short.

The problem for that team is how to cope with the other team's player advantage.

The problem for the team with the extra player is how best to capitalize on that advantage in the limited time available to square the match or win it.

Young players should be given frequent opportunities to solve such problems and to try out their own solutions. Teacher assistance is important; players' imaginations do need guidance.

(b) A team's goalkeeper is rather short and not at all confident when required to deal with high crosses. His punching technique is sound but his catching under pressure less secure.

The problem is how to reduce or even eliminate the possible exposure of the goalkeepers weaknesses.

The problem for the attacking side is how to expose and capitalize on those weaknesses.

(c) A team has no left footed players able to operate in normal mid-field or attacking roles.

The practice can be 'conditioned' so that no player in any of those roles may use his left foot to pass or kick the ball. If one does so he will give away a free kick.

The problem is to adapt team play to minimize any inconvenience or even to use the situation to advantage. How might the opposing team capitalize on and expose their opponents' limitations?

To extend conceptual problems and possibilities further and into more general considerations, how might deliberately playing wide attackers (wingers) on their 'wrong' sides, i.e. right footed players on the left side and so on, affect attacking play advantageously?

I recall Italy under master tactician Enzo Bearzot doing just that and to great effect. The 'different' long passing angles at the disposal of the wide players using their 'inside' feet set great problems for opposing full-backs and consequently to central defenders.

Not all players will be intrigued by these and similar problems: some will. However, all players should be challenged to develop their soccer intelligence by being persuaded to think about the game. One of the biggest problems besetting professional soccer in England has been the domination of thinking by team managers who want players only to do as they are told: until someone makes a mistake!

Mistakes, as is commonly known, are made by players, never by coaches!

Little wonder then that players facing problems in match play can't or won't think their way out of difficulties and are reluctant to try. If players are never encouraged to accept responsibility for their actions in practice, why should they do so in match play?

It is important to emphasize once more that soccer players do not learn, develop and improve predictably, nor do they develop according to age or physical maturity. Teachers and coaches can only watch for the signs which indicate a need and a readiness to learn and when those indications are clear to use them for all they are worth.

4.3 Practice.

Practice, to most people, means simply doing something over and over again and hopefully improving at it. 'Something', usually, is a muscular or whole body action and is described as a 'physical' skill mostly because it involves something which can be seen to happen as a result of movement. What is seen to happen, we hope, can be repeated with considerable and increasing accuracy as a result of practice.

A great deal of what passes for soccer practice relies more on hope than on expectation. For reasons best known to them, most sports teachers start at what they see as 'the bottom' and work upwards. In my view they might be much more successful if they started at the top and worked down!

What do we mean when trying to classify degrees of difficulty or mastery in skill by 'top' or 'bottom'? To start at the beginning we ought to clear our minds about skill, particularly about soccer skill.

4.31 What is Soccer Skill?

First things first. It will pay dividends to go back to the beginning of the chapter and re-examine the statement concerned with the definition of skill in soccer.

1. Soccer skill is the ability to play the game of soccer. And no one said anything about eleven a side soccer; at least not yet. Team soccer is the game of soccer, be it eleven a side or three versus three.

2. Soccer skill involves the use of a variety of less complex skills which I refer to as the techniques.

3. The techniques of the game are assembled and employed to enable players to construct combined (tactical) moves.

4. Soccer at its most sophisticated involves movements which do not necessitate contact with the ball although they may threaten to do so.

THE 'WHOLE' SKILL OF SOCCER AND ITS PARTS ARE EMPLOYED AS PERCEPTIVELY, ACCURATELY, SENSITIVELY AND AT SUCH SPEED AS MAY BE NECESSARY, INDIVIDUALLY OR WITH OTHER PLAYERS, TO OVERCOME OPPONENTS.

This is not splitting hairs or stating the obvious. It is important to understand what soccer skill really is if we are to make sense of preparing effective learning, teaching and practice situations.

Practice, obviously, is highly important in acquiring, refining and maintaining skill: at least the right sort of practice is. It is not enough for players merely to repeat what they have seen done by a teacher or what has been shown as 'good practice' by former players. There are accepted principles (precepts) which govern learning and practice.

(a) Skill, any skill, is highly specific.

Practice of any 'part' of the 'whole' skill in which improvement is sought, is likely to be relatively ineffective; the smaller the part the less the effectiveness. Similarly, practice of any other sport (skill) which has apparent resemblance to the 'target' skill will fail.

There is a widespread belief that we are born with a 'general' skill capability; a capability which can be applied in pursuit of excellence in all (or most) sports skills. It is thought that those so advantaged can achieve skillfulness almost certainly beyond the reach of those less fortunate; the belief is attractive but mistaken.

There may be inherited, genetic factors which affect the development of soccer skill. . . or any sports skill. . . reaction speed: depth perception: peripheral vision: height: acute hearing and so on. Inborn factors, in my view, are insignificant alongside an intense, enduring commitment to learning through imitation and play experience commenced at very early ages and carried on often into adulthood.

Intelligent, perceptive teaching and coaching with high degrees of motivation is the icing on that particular cake.

(b) The best way of practicing to improve at soccer is to play soccer: a lot!

Unfortunately the game is so complex that learning through playing alone cannot guarantee the repetition of experience (practice) which difficult or new skills demand unless the commitment to daily practice is enormous. There are parts of the world where it still is; they are disappearing fast. In those countries children play so much every day that they acquire astonishing degrees of excellence in individual and team skills. Nevertheless only a few become highly skillful. The idea that all African countries are overflowing with world beating soccer players is wishful thinking but their natural wells of sports commitment and ability still work: England's dried up long ago.

Children spending six, seven, or more hours each day in soccer play and practice is common in Third World countries, in most parts of the western world it isn't. In Egypt, on Cairo's empty car parks, I have seen large groups of children playing kick about soccer well past midnight. I also know of professional soccer players who complain of fatigue if required to practice and train for three or four hours a day, five days a week.

Perhaps they would complain less if training and practice were better planned and more interesting. Come to think of it I could be hard pressed to find professional coaches, in the game's mother country, capable of occupying their players for three to four hours a day.

4.32 Effective Practice: Common Elements.

The game itself is the fundamental skill of soccer. Practice must contain all or as many of the elements present in the game of soccer as the players can cope with.

Teachers and coaches must understand this; it is vitally important.

The game is only eleven-a-side in formal competition within the rules of those governing the game. Reduced to its simplest form, it may involve one player playing against another: two playing against one or two against two and so on. A goalkeeper for one or both 'sides' is an optional extra. Goals of some kind are important but the rest of the game's laws, other than those which govern fair and unfair (skillful and unskillful) play, are strictly for the 'big' game.

The smallest game practice, containing all the elements of the 'big' game, thereby meeting the first criterion of effective practice, is three versus three play. In 3 v 3, the principles of play, fundamental to preceptual learning, can be taught much more effectively than in the full game.

There may be practice phases which, for special purposes, involve no opponents but they will be much less effective overall because of that omission. They may be necessary because our only way of teaching the technical and tactical skills upon which game skill depends, is by simplifying and controlling the learning situation. Practice can concentrate on less complex aspects of soccer skill, in ways which are manageable by the players and which lead to player success.

4.33 Practice By Objectives.

All practice should be 'objective' directed. Players should know and understand what and why they are required to practice and how practice fits in to the 'big' picture, which is the game itself.

4.331 Mapping Out Progress.

This big picture, or 'cognitive map' as it is known, is set out much like the picture inside the box containing a jig-saw puzzle. To assemble the various parts of the jig-saw successfully and quickly it is necessary to refer frequently to the big picture. In teaching and coaching the jig-saw picture is the game itself in its different forms, be they 3 v 3 or 11 v 11.

4.332 Progress Markers.

Players should not only see and understand how the map is set out, they must know precisely where they are on it at any time, how the teacher intends that they should negotiate the tricky bits successfully and where the various markers of progress are positioned.

A jig-saw may have a hundred or more pieces but when reassembling the parts, most of us bring together pieces which make a larger piece but still a piece considerably smaller than the whole picture. We then reassemble these larger pieces into even larger pieces or back into the 'whole' picture. Learning and teaching soccer should proceed on similar lines.

For example, attacking play is only a part, albeit a large part, of the whole picture: practice might well involve the whole team of eleven players.

Let us take as an example attacking play as developed between wide attackers and central strikers. In the big game it involves perhaps four players plus some in support; it doesn't involve the whole team.

The tactical relationship between, say, two central strikers is an even smaller part of the 'whole' and practice design will cater for this 'mini' situation.

Finally, deficiencies in players' technical skills (techniques) will necessitate relatively small group practice enabling a player to concentrate his attention on fundamental technical elements.

This is perceptual practice.

Within each level of practice there will be degrees of difficulty which may be used to help a player to overcome learning and practice problems.

Each level of practice and the practice degrees within a level will be referred back to the big picture regularly. It is fitting the pieces back into the whole picture which is the difficult but vitally important aspect of practice design and development.

4.34 Insight.

Skills are learned more readily when the learner is given reliable 'clues' as to how a technique, for example, will be best achieved in all conditions.

To do this a teacher will relate any proposed solution to the problem to relevant principles of play; this is preceptual learning.

Some soccer teachers get involved in the intricate detail of limb positions and which part of the body moves where and when. Others, former players usually, try to teach by describing what they, in their time, did and by providing a running commentary on what a player subsequently does. Either way, the player is lost in technical jargon beyond his comprehension: promptly and wisely he 'shuts off'.

Principles (precepts) which can be applied to key factors in performance make learning easier, quicker and more lasting.

For example, there are all manner of ways of kicking a soccer ball but the power applied to a ball through a kick is:

(a) A direct product of the length of the player's leg during the forward swing,

(b) The speed at which his foot is traveling at impact and

(c) The length of the time that his foot is in contact with the ball.

These principles affect the results of all methods of kicking a ball.

The principles involved in bringing a ball under control are:

(a) A player should move as close as possible to the ball's line of flight (approach).

(b) The controlling surface should be selected early.

(c) The controlling surface should be relaxed and withdrawn fractionally before the ball makes contact.

(d) Withdrawal of the controlling surface should continue until the ball loses forward momentum.

More detail may be verbiage; players need to be taught only the things which matter.

4.35 Repetition.

Practice involves executing a technique or a tactical move a number of times until the skill can be reproduced at will, confidently and accurately, in game conditions.

Some players need a lot of practice, others less. Some appear to learn by 'seeing' the required skill mentally: some by employing a kind of muscle imagination; they 'feel' the moves involved without necessarily executing the skill or the various movements used to make up the skill.

Practice involves high levels of concentration as players try to reproduce the required pattern of what are often highly complicated movements.

4.36 Duration.

Most people can manage about twenty minutes of intense concentration in any learning situation. The duration of soccer practice with a single objective and involving some teacher input, should rarely exceed twenty minutes, thirty at most, without a break or change of activity.

It is possible for a teacher to work on one theme or objective for longer than twenty to thirty minutes but peak concentration should not extend much beyond twenty minutes.

4.37 Spacing.

Frequently repeated short periods (twenty minutes) of practice, interspersed with rest periods or periods which involve a complete change of activity will be the most effective ways of managing skill learning as complex as soccer. These short periods of practice followed by rest or change are called 'spaced' practices.

4.38 Massing.

Practice of significantly longer duration than twenty minutes, sixty minutes say, is called 'massed' practice. There is some evidence to show that while 'spaced' practice provides the regular foundation for effective soccer teaching and practice, occasional periods of massed practice seem to reinforce the learning and skill development process. 'Occasional' might be as infrequently as once every one or two weeks. Trial and success will be the only way for a teacher to find out.

4.39 Mental Practice or Rehearsal.

Many players appear to reinforce the learning process by practicing mentally. They seem to run through a mental 'film' of what they are trying to achieve, over and over again. They have a capacity for 'seeing' what will be required and how they will perform certain skills or moves accurately and successfully. There is no evidence that mental practice of motor skills can replace actual practice but it does appear to enhance it.

Pre-performance rehearsal, i.e. limited mental practice, whereby a player imagines himself actually performing while identifying key elements executed perfectly, seems to enhance skill learning for some people.

I wrote earlier that some players acquire a power of 'realistic imagination' through which they can practice techniques alone and quite effectively. They visualize themselves, during practice, as if they were playing in an actual game. They create fantasy football worlds in fact which at the time of practice are very real. If imagination of this kind is acquired it can be taught, with the right sort of inspiration.

Inspiration, it must be repeated, is the bedrock of a teacher's business.

4.40 Feedback.

Reference has been made to the need for a map or jig-saw picture of what a player should be trying to achieve. The picture should show how he will progress and how he will be judged to have made progress along the way.

The provision of information about 'how he has done', commonly called 'feedback' or 'knowledge of results', must be given as soon as possible after practice: immediately after preferably.

Many sports teachers, particularly coaches, seem to believe that a continuing feed-in of information about players' performances during play or practice is effective; it is highly unlikely.

Such evidence as there is shows that persistent comments on performance while players are practicing or playing is at best unwanted and unproductive, at worst destructive. Touch-line puppet masters may gain ego inflation from string pulling but their players gain nothing other than embarrassment. Most players take no notice and those who do only become apprehensive about adverse comments. Their performances deteriorate rather than improve.

4.41 Recency.
The most recent practice trial and its result is the one most readily recalled by players.

The further 'back' a practice took place, the less readily what happened in it is recalled.

All practice periods should end with a successful 'run' or at worst a 'run' which is JUDGED to have been successful by the teacher. Players will accept teachers' judgments when mutual trust and respect has been established between them. If he loses (or fails to gain) a player's trust in his judgment a teacher has serious, maybe irremediable problems.

Practice objectives should always be clear to players but the standards by which they will be judged are set by the teacher; they must be attainable.

4.42 Stepped Learning.
Learning does not proceed in a straightforward, predictable manner. The human organism needs periods of consolidation while it 'digests' the 'feed-in' of new information and experience and undertakes the internal reorganization which learning involves.

The so-called learning curve is not so much a curve as a series of steps, like a staircase: periods of climb are followed by periods when the player gathers himself (or herself) for the next upward thrust. Forcing progress, beyond the stepped limits of capability, will be unrewarding and even, occasionally, harmful.

Excessive practice or teacher input, at the wrong time, can cause serious 'indigestion' in the skill development process. Persistent indigestion, in this sense, is depressing.

The whole business of learning and practice must be founded upon reasonable, not great, expectations, similarly with teacher input. An over enthusiastic teacher can 'force feed' his players with information; give them too much to take in at once. This is a common fault with capable teachers, new to the job, faced with receptive players.

A member of my national coaching staff, eventually one of the best half dozen coaches I have ever seen, told me that in his first job with professionals he had taught them all that he knew inside six months!

4.43 Regression.
Learning is not a predictable phenomenon, sometimes players seem to go backwards in skill; they get worse before they resume progress. This is particularly noticeable among young players. Almost certainly it arises out of the 'skill indigestion' process referred to earlier. Teaching may have proceeded normally and practice successfully, with no sign of excessive 'feed in' but the player's receptive capability goes into reverse. Remedial treatment may require a complete break from practice and from the game, perhaps even the take-up of an activity totally removed from soccer or even from sport in general. Players can fall out of love with the game or with anything to do with it from time to time. The greater the pressure applied to regain the lost commitment, the greater the likelihood of the condition becoming serious and even permanent.

4.44 Learning Momentum.
Learning continues after teaching and practice have stopped. Research has demonstrated that the internal re-organization which is part of skill learning and practice continues and that significant, measurable levels of improvement have been found to take place a good while after practice has ceased.

This 'momentum effect' has important implications for coaches rather than teachers. When and how to practice certain tactical moves, at set plays for example, is vital if doing so can guarantee improved rates of success.

A team practiced a certain tactical move intensely three days before a match. The practice was entirely 'shadow' and technical, with no opposition. Wide players, reaching the goal line, delivered crosses well beyond the far side of the goal area to incoming players who 'pulled back' short passes, ten yards or so, to attackers arriving late from positions well outside the penalty area. The players had no further practice before a match three days later. The move was remembered and repeated successfully to a very high degree in match conditions.

I make no particular claims other than to say that player motivation was very high and that they believed in the efficacy of practice whatever forms it took. Certainly the 'momentum effect' of training for track athletes, wherein physiological capacities continue to show measurable improvement a significant time after training has stopped, are well known.

4.45 Other Considerations.
(a) Retention.
There are sound reasons for believing that soccer skills once learned are retained for very long periods and recalled with relatively little refreshment practice; our skill memories are very enduring. There are also sound

reasons for the belief that skills learned over a long period of time will only deteriorate slowly when practice has ceased. Similarly, skill acquired relatively quickly following intense exposure to learning and practice deteriorate almost as quickly as they were acquired when practice stops. These and similar phenomena shouldn't be a surprise since the physiological adaptation to training follows a similar pattern to skill practice. For example, strength or endurance developed quickly tend to fall off equally quickly when training levels drop.

Human adaptation to any form of change seems best achieved slowly and steadily if the wish is to retain it. What is true for physiological condition, it seems reasonable to assume, is likely to be true for psychological conditions; we are, after all, one person.

Soccer teachers and coaches need to understand this, it should affect everything they do.

(b) Learning By Direct Experience.

Experiential learning is the cause of much controversy in soccer teaching and coaching. Those who only half believe (or don't believe at all) in teaching base their lack of commitment on a conviction that some of us are born to be soccer players. This is a myth.

Usually, in Britain, it emanates from outstanding players who taught themselves and don't much like the thought of anyone emerging who might be taught to be as skillful as they were. I mentioned earlier the enormous commitment of time to practice through play given by many children in the poorer parts of the world. These conditions provide natural breeding grounds for players. Very few players brought up in affluence become genuine world class players. Unfortunately, natural breeding grounds are disappearing rapidly, hence the need for superior soccer teaching and coaching.

Learning through direct experience depends upon a number of conditions.

    (1) The willingness and the capability to devote vast amounts of time to free play and practice between say five years of age and fifteen.

    (2) The availability of the free time and the climatic conditions to enable such practice to take place.

    (3) Other young players available with and against whom to play and practice.

    (4) The accessibility of space, however rough or restricted, on which to practice.

    (5) The accessibility of older, physically superior players against whom to test developing skills when the need to do so is felt and opportunities occur.

    (6) The encouragement of inspirational models (usually older people)

for whom the developing player has high regard and through whom he can assess his developing talent and shape his aspirations.

Quite why or how very young players are seized by a desire to master new and complex soccer skills is not easy to say. The satisfaction of kicking and manipulating a ball and the approval gained for early success at it, are important factors in early 'bonding' with the game. Suddenly an obsessive commitment to the game takes unshakable hold.

Teachers privileged to come into contact with these 'driven' youngsters should avoid telling them what to do: just set them problems. Even when such players appear to be doing something wrong, think twice before correcting them. Talented, highly self-motivated young players should be given suggestions, or provoked or challenged but rarely given explicit instructions. . . I never say never!

Talented players know far more about their own capabilities than most teachers will ever know; their ambitions are unlimited. They need guidance on a very loose rein by being given problems to solve or shown how to be more different and even more successful. Their ideas of success may not be the teacher's.

These players are the game's gems who could become jewels. Teachers' and coaches' main task is to free these players from dependence on anyone. At quite early stages of development they should be deliberately educated to begin to teach and coach themselves; that means thinking through their own problems for themselves.

This flies in the face of those teachers and coaches who see themselves in absolute control of young players' soccer development. Puppet players eventually have to be set free but at that time they may have no idea how to use their freedom. The shock of having to stand on their own feet, to think and do things for themselves out of their own judgment may cause them to stop playing, forever.

Chapter 5
The Game

5.1 Playing Styles: Implications for Teachers and Players.

Why should children and young people play soccer and more importantly why should they be taught to play it?

What does the game provide or what should it provide which makes it
an attractive recreational prospect? What special opportunities does
soccer present as a suitable vehicle for education?

How should the game be played, taught and coached so that while
retaining its magnetism for players it is also socially,ethically and educa-
tionally acceptable?

Clearly the game as played world wide by professionals is a very influential consideration not least because television provides sustained,intense
exposure for past, present and future generations of soccer people but is
that exposure beneficial?

All sports rely for inspiration on current models and those who influence
them: teachers, coaches, leaders and administrators.

Many have far reaching effects. Do those effects work in the best
interests of the game's future? Are today's teachers pursuing objectives in
player development which are less than compatible with what a media
dominated society wants the game to be?

These are important questions; they need to be answered by all who
seek to influence the way in which the game is played and the players who
play it.

5.11 Individuality.

Soccer was devised to meet the needs of a society which, in times of
enormous industrial and social upheaval, needed inspiration, release and
above all perhaps relief from life's increasing pressures. British industrial
society needed talismanic and escapist activities and found, in soccer, an
activity which embraced individual cleverness, tactical cunning and
athletic excellence within a set of rules devised by gentlemen for those
aspiring to join them. At the same time, the game provided for a new trib-
alism which, in its rural form, the industrial revolution almost destroyed.

Soccer was and should be a simple game to play, capable of generating
enormous pleasure even when played badly.

Crucially, the game was welcomed with open arms by those with high
aspirations for the 'education for all' movement which,in turn, had its
roots deep in the fundamentals of the new Lutheran Christianity of the
time. Soccer was heaven sent, almost literally, for the benefit of Christian

teachers and their schools.

Soccer became everything to everyone: the game of the people, played by the people, for the benefit of the people: all of them!

Whatever is done in the names of winning and professionalism by the world's great soccer nations and clubs, teachers must never forget their responsibility for protecting the pleasure derived from skill in what has been rightly described as 'the world game'.

Without the beauty of expressionist skills the game, at all levels, could be in serious decline; it may be moving in that direction.

Insatiable demands for success are eroding the place of individual skill. The danger is that as top teams embrace 'win at all cost' beliefs they are imitated by often ill-trained teachers and coaches, themselves infected by the 'win at all costs' virus. A cure must be found. Unless young players well into adolescence are positively required to develop and use individual skill, in competitive matches and in recreational play, players capable of reshaping the game will be gone forever. It will not be enough to encourage individuality when it occurs. Players must be positively required to play with as much individuality as they can be taught and encouraged to achieve. And individuality doesn't mean unrestricted selfishness. A selfish player does everything for personal pleasure and reward. Individuality enables players to play differently, even extravagantly differently while recognizing the needs for co-operative play and team achievement.

Individual skills allow a player to combine with other individually, skillful players differently and excitingly. Only players with individual skills and individual thinking can change the game and take it forward and they will not be produced from repetitive practice of the orthodox or by reducing the game to a set of statistically conceived patterns.

5.12 Style.

Playing style should reflect a coming together of what the players and teachers (and coaches) have agreed is their most appealing and enjoyable way of playing the game. Winning matches without the enjoyment of playing is the antithesis of sport.

Examples of two extremes in style might be as follows:

Team 'A's play is based upon sustained athletic commitment with the employment of individual and team skill shaped and governed by that commitment. To avoid losing, they stop their opponents from playing before attempting to win themselves. They apply heavy pressure against opponents in all parts of the field but especially in mid-field from where attacking play traditionally developed momentum; at least it did until mid-field play makers became the objects of physical abuse.

Team 'A' has a DIRECT style.The ball is always projected along the shortest possible route to the opposing goal.

DIRECT play demands FUNCTIONAL EFFICIENCY from the individual players,all of them: all of the time! Players are required to use only those techniques which contribute to DIRECT, FUNCTIONAL EFFICIENCY.

Imaginative, creative, EXPRESSIVE play is the antithesis of effective play.

Team B's play is based upon the employment of individual skill accurately, perceptively and deceptively. Although fully aware of opponents' strengths, they are more concerned with positive exploitation of opponents' weaknesses. They defend to gain and use possession until a shooting chance can be created with high certainty. They only put possession at risk to make shooting and scoring opportunities.To achieve shooting positions, Team 'B' adopts a VARIABLE PRESSURE, INDIRECT approach to opponents' goals. INDIRECT play and VARIABLE PRESSURE play allows players optimum time and space in which to use individual skills precisely and with considerable individual choice.

Players are encouraged to EXPRESS themselves in skill selection and considerable store is set by DECEPTIVE play. Team 'B' is prepared to accept the possibility of giving goals away in order to increase their chances of scoring.

Having made a conscious decision about style,a coach and his team can then set out and sort out their skill development priorities. Out of those priorities will come, logically, priorities for planning all coaching and training routines short and long term. And out of that kind of logic will come accurate estimates of the resources needed for development to be effective.

Team 'A' should allocate a relatively high proportion of preparation time to physical conditioning, especially to endurance:speed training. That will give them the capacity for sustained athletic commitment. Organization through full team practice will feature prominently in their preparation; practice which will aim to improve the unified and simplified commitment of the team as a whole. Skill practice will be highly 'co-operative' and methodical. Players will practice limited functional skills to attain high degrees of efficiency in their employment.

Team 'B' will spend much of its preparation time on polishing existing individual skills and encouraging, through practice and coaching, new ones. Two, three and four player combination possibilities and responsibilities will be practiced in detail. Physical conditioning will be aimed at speed and agility developed in close conjunction with individual skills. Small sided game practice will feature prominently and initiative in all phases of play will be encouraged.

To my certain knowledge there are teams in England, identical with team 'A', who spend much of their preparation time on short passing, often intricate six or seven a-side play. They may or may not do a lot of running in training but where they do, much of it will be even paced distance work across country.

In competition, however, what they practiced in small sided games is forbidden.

All black and mid-field players launch the ball high and far distant towards and hopefully beyond opposing defenders. Forward attackers pursue these passes doggedly and optimistically.

That sort of logic produces an almost unbelievable conflict of interests between preparation and play, is good, but usually has unanswered questions.

Style, not strategy is the foundation for everything done in the names of teaching and coaching in soccer. Ask players to play in a style incompatible with the way in which they were raised and a team has serious, almost irreparable problems: deservedly so in my view.

5.13 Ethics and The Laws of The Game.
Having agreed on a playing style, a team must agree on its' interpretation of the game's laws and how that interpretation should affect attitudes to opposing players, to referees and to illegal practices. Clearly, team A's style and methods will occasion significantly more body contact with opponents than will team B's. Sustained power and confrontational athletic commitment, together with a significant limited range of personal skills, make that inevitable.

Body contact is legal in soccer so long as it observes the conditions specified in Law 12. Outside those conditions deliberate, illegal body contact is cheating.

Of course, the mere speed and therefore reduced skillfulness of team A will make contact with other players barely avoidable, intentional or otherwise. Intention is the operative but controversial word.

Referees must start from the premise that soccer is a game of skill. If in doubt, their decisions must always favor the player who is trying to be skillful. Interpreting the intentions of opponents towards that player, almost impossible to achieve in top class soccer, is simplified.

A referee's first responsibility must be to protect skillful players from illegal, unskillful or careless play.

The duty of team A's coaches is now clear, to practice their limited ranges of techniques at speed without making contact with opponents; I'll wager that few if any do.

In fact they cheat by omission and they should be dealt with as the cheats they undoubtedly are. 'NUDGE AND WINK' illegalities or 'sharp practices', seen as jokes in the professional game, are seriously damaging to the game's health; they must be ruthlessly eliminated.

5.2 The Principles of Individual Play.

There are certain principles, or precepts if you wish, which influence success in soccer to the extent that sticking to them, generally speaking, is more likely to bring success than if they are ignored.

Principles do not guarantee success but they are the basis upon which sensible individual and team play are founded and upon which effective teaching becomes possible.

'Reading' a game, as is different from studying individual players, is impossible without understanding soccer's principles.

5.21 Attacking.

Applied to attacking or counter attacking play these principles are,

- (a) To contribute to team possession by developing those skills by which ball possession can be kept and used to the greatest advantage.
- (b) To create and take shooting opportunities by dribbling,passing or moving to receive the ball past, between or over opponents.
- (c) To deliver the ball to other players better positioned and able to use it to greater effect in making or taking shooting chances.
- (d) To pass and move into pass receiving positions nearer to the opponents' goal whenever possible and consistent with remaining onside.
- (e) To draw opponents away from the most profitable shooting areas and away from other attackers positioned in or near to them.
- (f) To put ball possession at risk only near to the opponents' goal or in moves calculated to move the attack there and especially where the probability of shooting chances are enhanced.
- (g) To set opponents difficult marking problems.
- (h) To create space for other players.
- (i) To seek to regain possession of the ball positively, particularly near to the opposing goal.

Players in attack which, increasingly, means all ten outfield players, must be taught to 'see' the game, especially its attacking possibilities, from different positional view points. The days when players were attackers or defenders according to where they were positioned on the team sheet or on the field are long gone. As individualism has diminished, the need for all round players has increased. Today, players must attack and defend as the flow of play and opportunities demand. The sooner they are taught the implications of this development the better for the game.

5.22 Defending.

Defending is so much easier than attacking: dangerously so. Excessive attention paid to stopping other players from playing effectively, at early ages, could be the death of the game as it was originally conceived; the threat may be greater than we think.

Young players should be introduced to individual defensive principles no earlier than twelve or thirteen years of age and to the principles of team play not much before fifteen years.

Principles are not tactics but that's what they tend to become when team results over-ride the need for individual development.
Individual defending principles are as follows:

(a) opposing attackers should be marked or tracked increasingly closely as they and the ball move forward.
*Tracking an opponent means watching and following an opponent's changes of position at a distance.

(b) to seek to regain ball possession safely and surely by developing the skills of intercepting,tackling and marking.

(c) to block shots at goal when threatened and to prevent the ball being passed into advantageous shooting positions.

(d) to contain individual opponents with the ball by restricting their action options and guiding them into safe areas.

(e) when not required to mark, to cover other defenders or move forward to threaten to challenge opponents with the ball.

(f) to maintain an integrated defensive relationship with other players by refusing to be drawn away from such relationships unless extreme circumstances demand it.

(g) to force opponents into taking risks with possession of the ball.

(h) to minimize the space and time available for an opponent to make decisions.

(i) to challenge, mark or otherwise contain any attacker moving towards goal and behind other defenders, with or without the ball.

To some coaches defense is very attractive; they enjoy the negative and destructive side of the game. I can't object to that if defense is used to set up attacking play. Where defense is practiced for its own sake, as part of a 'no risk' playing style then that is the worst kind of negative play and is completely unprincipled. It's not the business teachers should be in.

With the ball, a team must try to score goals.

Without the ball, a team must seek to get it to try to score goals.

Attack of course can be negative: when ball possession is used unimgi- natively and with minimal risk and when excessive numbers of players are held behind the ball unnecessarily.

Professional soccer, world wide, is often dominated by cautious or negative tactical play. Those in doubt should count the number of 'on target' shots at goal in their next televised match.

Individuality is the foundation of excellence in team performance.The greater the limitations of each individual's skill, the less a team's capabilities for producing the unexpected, decisive move and the more predictable that team's playing methods become.

Limited individual players limit a team's strategical and tactical options. Team tactics have to accommodate players' deficiencies before positive objectives can be pursued.

5.3 Teaching the Principles of Attack and Defense.

The principles of individual play lead logically to the principles of match play, those of attack and defense. Individual players' talents and skills are integrated into coherent team performance, performance which makes the best possible use of individual skill to enhance the performance of the team.

Teaching soccer in relation to these principles is best left until players fully understand the precepts of individual play and are ready to move on to a more complete understanding of how everyone's part fits into the 'whole' picture, ie. the full game.

When coaching I would demonstrate the application of the principles in 11 v 11 games. In teaching, I would use at most 6 v 6 play and most often 3 (plus a goalkeeper) v 3.

5.31 Ball Possession.

When ball possession is lost, opponents have opportunities to score.

The nearer to their own goal players are when possession is lost, the greater the likelihood of opponents scoring.

Of course, unless a team in possession puts the ball at risk in certain parts of the pitch, it is unlikely to score.

Possession of the ball, which could increase attacking and scoring options, should rarely be used for no better purpose than keeping it.

(a) Teaching Possession Play.

Players: Six, seven year old players
Area: 40 yds. x 30
5 v 1 'keep ball'. The 'five' try to achieve a target number of passes e.g. 20, before the 'one' is changed. If the 'one' intercepts the ball he replaces the player who allowed the interception.

Where the ball goes out of play, the player who caused it to do so replaces the 'one' in the middle.

As practice becomes easy, the area may be reduced or the 5 v 1 changed to 4 v 2.

Different shapes of the practice area, 60 yds. x 20 for example, will cause different problems for possession players.

Playing 'conditions' can be imposed to increase difficulty.

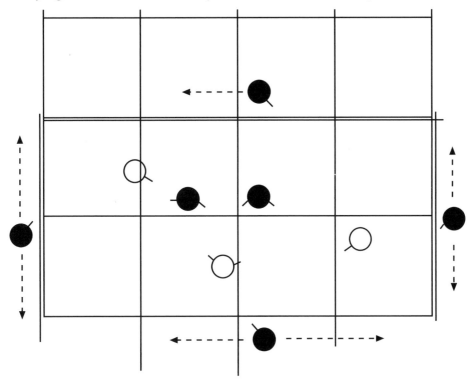

Diagram 19. *'Keep' Ball.*

Conditions.
   (1) No player may touch the ball more than three times (or twice) before passing.
   (2) Each of the 'five' must control the ball with one foot and pass it with the other.
   (3) Each of the 'five' must only touch the ball with one foot.

Eventually we need to change from pure possession play to a more perceptive skill,
   (4) In 4 v 2 the four try to score 20 points without interruption. Any pass scores one point but a pass between or over the 'two' scores three points if possession is maintained.

The incentive emphasizes the need for selecting positive passing opportunities WITHOUT BEING CAUGHT DOING SO.

The element of deception of pretending to take one option but taking another, must be introduced very early in soccer life.

Deceptive players are worth their weight in gold; in professional soccer they often cost that much.

If players adapt quickly to practice, their skill can be challenged by reducing the practice area to 30 yards x 20.

Practice numbers reduced to 3 v 3 may be beyond the capabilities of very young players although they are likely to enjoy trying. Better, but still testing, would be seven players playing 3 v 3 with the fourth player always joining the side in possession of the ball to make 4 v 3.

Our medium term aim is to move practice increasingly towards actual game circumstances.

The teams play 3 v 3 where one team with the ball is trying to keep the ball to score against the other team one of whose players must be the temporary goalkeeper. Effectively this becomes a 3 v 2 practice but so does the game itself with skillful players. The main tactical purpose of the game played at any level is to create 2 v 1, 3 v 2 or any situation in which the attackers temporarily outnumber defenders.

In diagram 19, the five players are 3 v 2 inside the area (40 yds. x 20). When an interceptor is successful he and his partner try to make three consecutive passes to the players outside the area. The other three inside the area try to regain possession.

'Outside' players cannot enter the area but can move round it; 'inside' players cannot leave it.

Ball possession allows a team to determine where, how and at what speed the game will be played. The speed of play is determined by the speed at which the ball is moved from player to player.

To speed up play effectively, it is necessary, first, to slow it down. Similarly to slow play down it is advantageous, to first speed it up. It is the change of speed rather than speed itself which causes problems for opposing teams. And the secret of sustaining possession and thereby controlling play, is to have an extra player in all parts of the field; the implications of that statement are worth thinking about.

5.32 Position.

In possession of the ball a team can either counter attack instantly and directly, thereby creating a surprise condition, or it can move the ball rather more slowly and with less risk into the opponents' half of the field and try to make shooting chances from there.

If possession is lost during a quick counter attack, those deployed in attacking positions may not respond as quickly as needed to loss of possession. Mentally they may still be attacking when physically they should be defending. A team committed to building up a strongly supported, forward, attacking position, dependent on control rather than speed, will be less vulnerable to quick counter attacks. Having moved the ball into a forward attacking position, a team should be prepared to work hard to keep play there. When, at what speed and how far they should fall back is a matter of tactics based upon player strengths or weaknesses. That is really a coaching matter and a fairly sophisticated one at that.

To counter attack with surprise and at speed a team needs space behind their opponents into which to run and pass the ball.

A defending team may deliberately draw their opponents forward by falling back (retreating) in front of the ball before seeking to counter attack. How far they retreat is a matter of tactical judgement.

In diagram 20, the black team has withdrawn into its own half where it begins to defend positively by putting opponents under pressure especially near to the ball. Should possession look like being regained the players furthest away from the ball will seek 'blind side' positions against their nearest opponents, taking care to remain onside. When possession is regained, those near to the ball will know that those furthest away in forward positions will be looking for quickly released passes into space behind the defenders and out of reach of the goalkeeper. This last consideration is important; goalkeepers are often required to operate outside their penalty areas as auxiliary 'sweeper' backs.

5.33 Surprise.
As shown previously, attacking play should have an element of surprise. Consistent with players' passing accuracy and range of passing techniques, long and short, aerial or on the ground, attackers should try to hide their intentions: where to strike: where to move players to overcome defenses: when and where the final thrust will be made to break through and shoot. Surprise is most effectively created when players from unusual team positions break forward into attack.

Soccer's future rests in the hands. . . at any rate the feet. . . of all-round players, players capable of and willing to function effectively in any position on the field.

5.34 Depth in Attack. (Triangulation)
The disposition of any three players in attack should present the player 'on' the ball with all-round passing opportunities.

In diagram 21, black players are more or less in line across the pitch. Black 7, with the ball, can only pass to one player, Black 8, with confidence. Players, 9, 10 and 11 cannot be reached easily or safely, Black 8 is blocking black 7's passing lines.

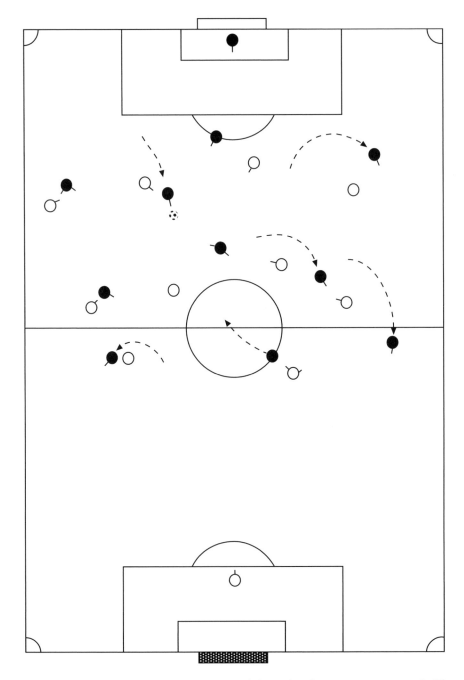

Diagram 20. *Retreating to set-up pressure defense leading to counter attack. The need for 'blind-side' positioning.*

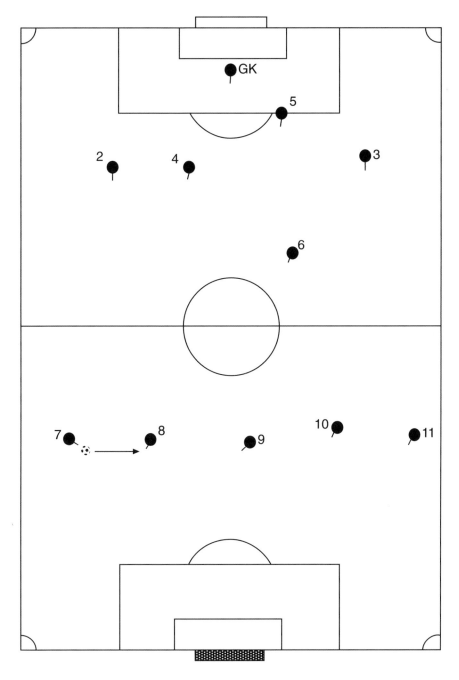

Diagram 21. *Flat attack.*

In diagram 22, the triangles produce all-round passing options for Black 7.

If Black 8, 9 and 10, without the ball, continually move forward, sideways and back in circular patterns, while retaining the triangular relationship, they will produce good passing options and make marking very difficult. Players are often exhorted by coaches to 'pass and move', only rarely are they told where to move or when and even more rarely, why. Attackers should try to pass and move towards the opposing goal, preferably when no defender is looking. Having made a forward move, if the attacker is picked up and marked he should continue his movement away from goal. Players who pass and stand still cause team play to become static.

Immovable attackers make defending generally and close marking in particular very easy.

Triangulation is extended by adding players singly or in groups to form interlocking triangular patterns according to tactical requirements.

The effectiveness of a triangular pattern is determined by the responsibility each player shows towards the other players in the group and the distances between them. The greater the distance the less their abilities to support each other against opposing pressure. The 'flatter' the triangle the less advantageous certain passing angles and options become.

5.35 Penetration.

Having used controlled possession to establish position, a team will attack effectively when players see and take advantage of opportunities to run the ball (dribble) or pass it behind (through or over) opposing defenders and into ultimate or penultimate shooting positions.

Penetration is most probable where a significant number of attacking players constantly seek positions from which they can win any race to receive passes between, over and behind defenders without moving offside.

Penetrative passes have to be delivered deceptively, accurately and with the appropriate 'weight'.

Penetration is certainly more likely when a number of attackers move into and out of forward receiving positions almost continuously. Their movements stop when one of them finds a position in which he could receive a pass, turn and shoot or free himself briefly from close marking.

Reference has been made to the importance of 'blind-side' positions in attack, positions which find a defender between a probable pass receiver and the player with the ball. All players, whatever their 'team sheet' positions, should practice moving into blind side positions unnoticed. If blind side positions achieve nothing more, they cause defending players to pay increased attention to individual opponents than they might otherwise

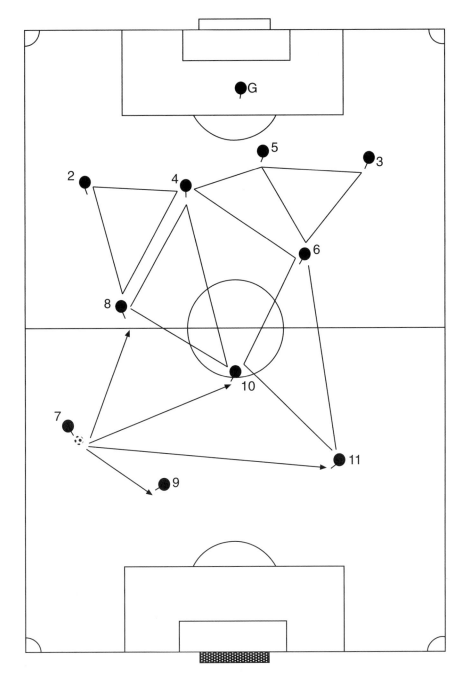

Diagram 22. *Triangulation to produce useful supporting angles and distances.*

seek to do.

Effective defending relies on a number of players sharing responsibilities for marking, covering and challenging in highly integrated forms. It's difficult to attend to these responsibilities while a single opponent's position and movement is the cause of concern.

5.36 Dispersion.

Dispersion means spreading out. The further that attackers move apart, the more they are likely to take defenders with them and the more space they create for each other. Of course 'stretching' team positions bears the risk of taking players out of the range of their teammates' passing skills and away from positions in which two or more players could support each other. A great deal of energy, in top class soccer, is spent in minimizing the space which attackers have in which to play. Preventing opponents from playing, by allowing them no space and therefore no time, is the sole strategical purpose of many teams. The distance between backs and strikers is squeezed, at most to thirty yards and the middle of the playing zone is populated by as many as ten players all the time.

'Play makers', those mid-field players traditionally responsible for creating shooting opportunities for strikers, are an endangered species.

In a 4 v 4 game, diagram 23, a playing condition is that, having given a pass, a player must run towards and outside the player to whom he has passed. Failure to do so concedes possession to the other team.

This conditioned practice serves at least two purposes; first it ensures that the receiver can depend on close support from at least one player and second, the movement tends to spread play out. Consequently it is likely to draw defenders away from central positions ie. in front of goal. If they refuse to be drawn, penetration is more likely possibilities are increased in the 2 v 1 situation created by what is called an 'over-lapping' or 'loop' run.

5.37 Mobility.

The practice in 5.36 will produce a certain amount of positional interchange or mobility. Mobility aims to unsettle the marking and distance relationships between defenders. It requires an understanding of basic defensive priorities, where the dangerous areas are and how they are likely to be defended.

In diagram 24, the shaded area is that from which effective shots are most likely. Defenders will concentrate in and on the central edge of that area: less so towards the sides where shooting angles become more difficult. Attackers' movements will have the following objectives:

(1) to draw defenders away from goal.

(2) to enlarge the spaces between defenders,especially between central defenders.

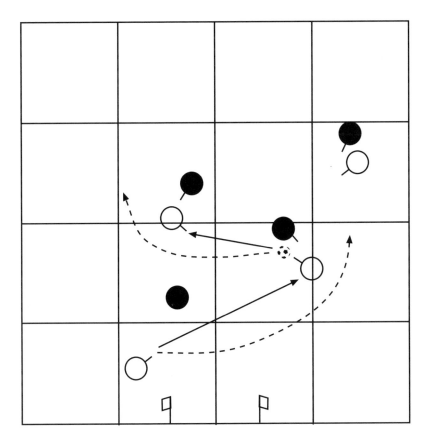

Diagram 23. *Attacking support from overlapping runs.*

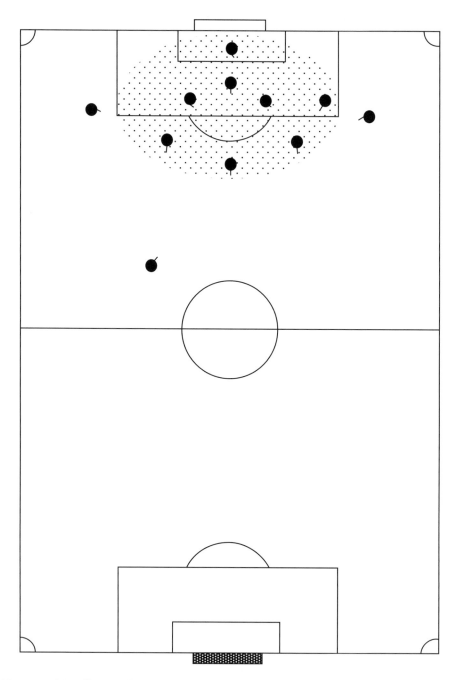

Diagram 24. *Effective shooting area showing possible concentration of defenders.*

(3) to distract key defenders, thereby enabling surprise attackers to be freed for shots or for inter-passing moves leading to shots.

(4) to disturb defenders' concentration and to create anxiety.

(5) to establish numerical superiority (2 v 1 and so on), however briefly, to enhance interpassing possibilities through tight defenses.

Modern soccer, emphasizing heavy defensive strategies, needs players who are mobile, who are comfortable in different positions and who move in and out of those positions surely and with complete understanding.

5.38 Deception.

Risking the accusation of repetition I must repeat that players who are limited in their range of skills can never be as deceptive as those with fewer limitations.

It doesn't take much insight to recognize the serious tactical limitations which accrue from a player's inability to play with one foot. In a well briefed, professional team players will adjust angles of approach to a one-footed opponent to compel him to use his 'bad' foot. Subsequent pressure will find him lacking enough double-footed skill to get him out of trouble. If he is a defender, players nearby must make major positional adjustments to help him resolve his (and their) problem.

The sooner that problems posed by one footed players are addressed, the better for the game. Some pro soccer coaches argue that it is more profitable to concentrate on making the good foot even better while using the bad one exclusively for standing on. That is nonsensical rubbish. The first requirement for individual deception is good two footedness. Secondly, with or without the ball, he should be able to hide his intentions until he actually plays the ball or makes his move.

5.4 Basic Tactical Skills.
5.41 Running The Ball And Dribbling.

A player with the ball can either run it towards or away from opponents.

His choice is a matter of tactics. If he runs it towards a heavy concentration of opponents his intentions are likely to be to draw those defenders into even tighter relationships so that he can play the ball wide to teammates much less heavily opposed. Diagram 25.

If he runs the ball away from opponents his intentions will be to pull one or more opponents away from others, thereby loosening the defensive structure. Diagram 26.

Knowing his own strengths and weaknesses, an attacker, running the ball at a defender, will run, initially, towards that side of a defender which takes the attacker towards his poorer side (and probably towards the defender's better one): let's say the attacker's left. Moving towards the left

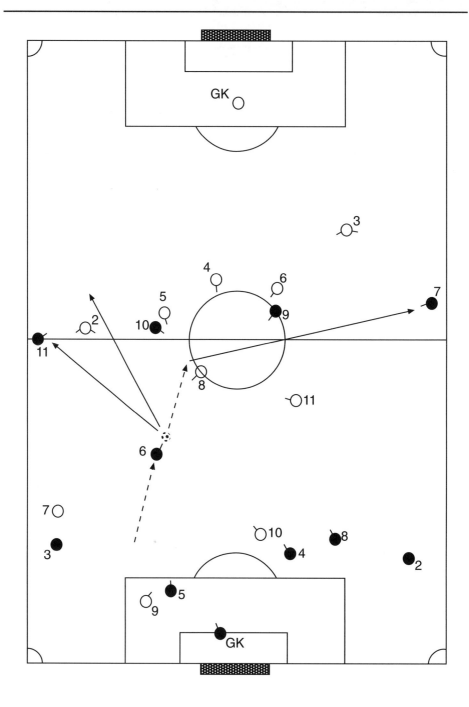

Diagram 25. *Running the ball towards congested central areas preparatory to passing to wide attackers in space.*

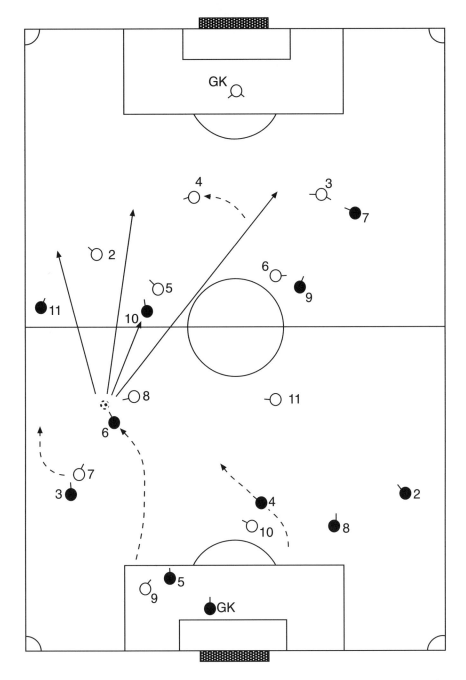

Diagram 26. *Running the ball away from central defensive concentration to loosen the defense and to make space.*

will cause most defenders to move in the same direction thereby unbalancing them against a dribbling 'break' in the opposite direction ie. to the attacker's right and on to his 'good foot'.

A player clearly attacking an opponent on one particular side is, or should be, signalling teammates for support on the other side. Diagram 27.

Running the ball across the penalty area and deliberately at one of his own players, the runner may be working for a shooting opening by creating a situation in which he can go on to shoot or leave the ball behind for his teammate. Dribbling across defenders inevitably draws some or all of them into following the movement of the player in possession or at least into watching it. Defenders persuaded to watch the ball can be exposed to all sorts of attacking possibilities.

5.42 Reversing Play.

Running in one direction and passing in the opposite direction also unbalances defenders, especially, as we have seen, near to the opposing penalty area. Near to the penalty area, defenders know that attackers need very little space in which to shoot. Shots or even threats of shots must be taken seriously and blocked. Two defenders, in these situations, are often drawn into doing the same job; both adjust positions to threaten an assumed shooting attempt. Diagram 28.

In these circumstances a short, reverse pass is likely to create a better shooting opportunity for an attacker moving in the opposite direction to the dribbling player and to the defenders moving to block him. Any attacker, unsure where to move to assist an attacking development, could do worse than to move in a direction opposite to the flow of the attack.

5.43 Losing Markers.

Soccer at its simplest is a one against one player struggle.It becomes 2 v 1 or 5 v 4 when tactics are organized to eliminate the possibility of any one player proving to be too skillful for his opponent. Rather than teach and coach a player to improve his individual capabilities, many coaches reorganize team play so that defending players link up and accept full responsibility for one opponent and part responsibility for another;this is called 'splitting' opponents. Losing or evading a marker is an important tactical skill. It depends on a player's constant sense of where danger is likely to threaten and how (and when) an opposing defender must relax his attention to one opponent in the interests of collective defensive security. A clever attacker will often encourage his marker towards the defending positions the marker prefers. At the moment when the defender dare not leave his position, the attacker will pull away slightly leaving his marker with two choices, to stay or to follow, either of which may be

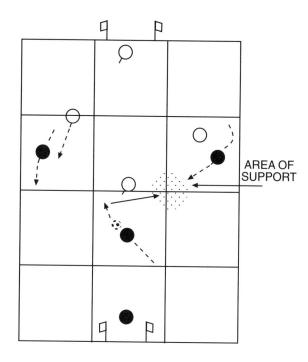

Diagram 27. *3 v 3 running the ball against one side of a defender to signal the expectation of support on the opposite side.*

AREA OF SUPPORT

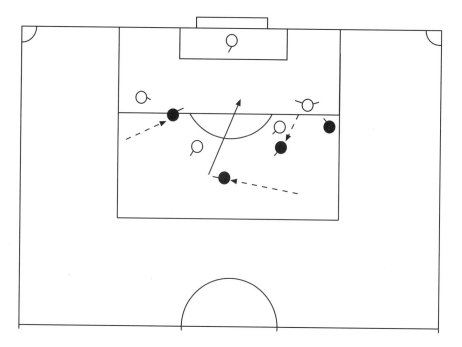

Diagram 28. *4 v 4 in an open 40 X 40 yards moving across the penalty area to draw defenders away from the target area for a reverse pass.*

wrong; it's called catching an opponent in two minds.

Markers can also be lost when they are drawn to watch what is happening near to the ball (ball watching). An attacker will watch his marker's eyes until he is confident that the player is ball watching, at which time the attacker 'fades' out of sight behind and away from his opponent.

In high class soccer I have seen a player lose a marker by standing still! Marked touch-tight and with the probability that it would last for the whole game Holland's great mid-field player, Johann Cruyff, took up a position between his strikers and mid-field and stayed there apparently totally dispirited at the prospect of being man-marked out of the game. Eventually his marker felt confident enough about Cruyff's submission to contribute to his team's general play and relaxed his marking commitment. Cruyff immediately 'took off', never to be 'caught' again and proceeded to destroy the opposition.

1 v 1 practices should play a major part in the development of all young players, especially when they show a genuine appreciation of the importance of group (team) play. 1 v 1 presents teachers with opportunities to show players how to deal with individual opponents.

An attacker, having moved past an opponent, will learn to run the ball directly at goal to shoot because he has no one to pass to.

Passing, in common with most things in life, can be considerably overdone.

In 5 v 5 practice where players with or without the ball are taught tight marking, any player with the ball and having beaten one opponent is likely to have no one immediately available to pass to. He must run the ball: strongly and directly and preferably towards goal.

Soccer isn't simply a passing game; played well, it's a dribbling, passing and shooting game and a clever one at that.

Players must learn how to take on and defeat individual opponents in attack by running the ball cleverly or strongly, preferably both, towards goal. That's how most of us learn to play the game anyway.

5.44 'Showing' the Ball.

Whenever receiving or in possession of the ball a player should try to 'show' opponents what he intends to do with it but with no intention of doing so! If he needs to control the ball in the air with his chest, say, he should give every sign that he intends to head it. If he wants to control a pass and move left, a player should give all the preparatory signs of passing to someone on his right. Having signalled a pass, he must then have the skill to change to a controlling movement before moving right.

All technical practice should include the additional technique of 'showing' a different intention before employing the technique selected. Even with very young players, the proposition of pretense should be put to them. If nothing else it will persuade some of them, at some time in the future, to at least think about the possibility of practicing deceit; a few may take to the idea immediately.

It is important that body language gives all the genuine signs of 'correctness'; exaggerated fake moves, overacting, fool no one.

'Fake' moves are absolutely fundamental to successful dribbling. An intended dribbling 'break' to the left will be preceded by a convincing signal of a move to the right. A feint to play the ball with the inside of the right foot changes to a foot movement over the ball and a break with the outside of the same foot in the opposite direction.

Highly skillful players have the special 'body language', the use of which gives opponents highly convincing but totally confusing signals of intent. Sometimes no more than a quick glance in a certain direction is enough to send opponents moving the same way and wrongly more often than not.

'Body swerve' is the ability to sway almost the whole of the body, from the ankles upwards, in one direction to 'throw' opponents off balance as they try to counter the move. Having begun to swerve one way the player swerves in the other direction in almost the same movement.

If the ability to send out 'fake' signals is used with either outstanding speed or change of speed, players become almost unstoppable when sending their opponents 'the wrong way'.

5.45 Return Passing (Wall Pass).

This, the simplest and most fundamental form of inter-passing skill, involves two players: at the game's highest levels three.

In 4 v 4 practice (area: 50 yds. x 30) a game condition is that, having given a pass a player must move towards that player to take a return pass.

A successful return pass scores two points.

If he collects the return pass behind an opponent he scores four points.

If the return pass leads to a shot at goal he scores a bonus four points for his team.

Each team's goalkeeper can become an outfield player while his team is in possession of the ball. When possession is lost he must return to his goal line, quickly.

The extra player in attack should create many possibilities for 2 v 1 situations leading to return passing moves.

Where three players combine, two may set up a return pass possibility but it is the third player, moving beyond opponents, who should receive the ball.

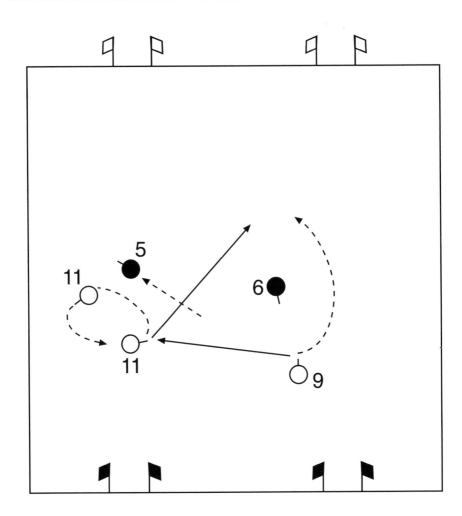

Diagram 29. *Moving to break down cover and to use a wall pass.*

5.46 Making Space.

At early stages in development players will only be concerned with getting the ball and they will be dissatisfied when they don't. Their dissatisfaction will increase if, on the rare occasions when the ball does arrive, another player arrives at the same time and steals it.This is the situation which a perceptive teacher will use to present a case for learning moves to gain more space in which to secure possession of the ball.

In diagram 29, the players are playing 3 v 2 (area 40 yds. x 20). The 'goals', two at each end, are three yards wide.There are no goalkeepers.

A goal is scored by passing the ball between the 'goal posts'.

White 11, without the ball, moves away from white 9, who has the ball, threatening to move behind his opponent, black 5.

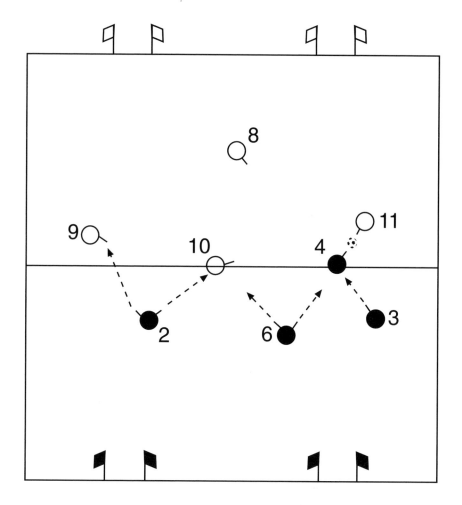

Diagram 29 (a). *White players in safe positions cannot affect the disposition of their opponents.*

White 11 changes direction quickly to move back towards his partner offering himself for a wall pass. White 11's move is to take away cover from black 6 and then to make space for a possible wall pass.

In diagram 29(a). An area 40 yds. x 40 goals as previously and no goalkeepers.

White 11 with the ball, is marked by black 4 and covered by blacks 3 and 6.

Black 2 is 'splitting' whites 9 and 10 and watching white 8 from a distance.

White players lingering in 'safe' positions cannot affect the disposition of their opponents: they will, when and if they move towards the opposing goal. Then, opponents must adjust their positions to counter the threats posed by the white players' forward moves. Eventually some or all of the black players must mark their white opponents.

At that time, any movement of white players towards goal must cause reactions in the black team. Then, white players are able to make space for each other, especially for the player with the ball, by attracting opponents into following them.

This is called 'picking up' (collecting) opponents and is vitally important in understanding how to move defenders and to make space for attacking moves, especially near to goal.

In diagram 30, at a corner kick, the shaded areas are those into which kicks should be aimed. Attackers will gain the greatest advantage where they can move into those areas late and on the run. It is essential that attackers take up starting positions away from target areas. They are likely to draw markers away from the same areas. Deception might involve taking up early positions in the key areas, in order to collect markers: moving out and then moving back into those areas very late as the ball is delivered.

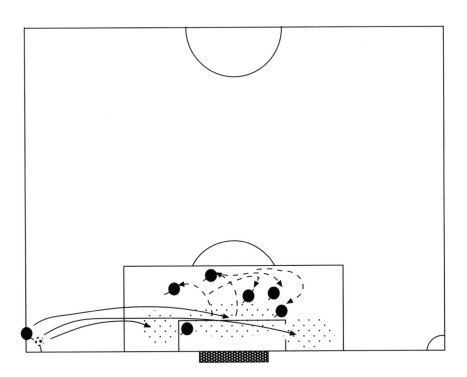

Diagram 30. *Emptying important space before attacking it late.*

5.47 Shooting Space.

Many teams strive to achieve shooting opportunities by moving the ball, dribbling, passing or crossing, in one direction only: forward.

This is the expected action: expected, by both defenders and attackers. Effective shots are more likely when, having moved forward, advanced attackers play the ball behind them for supporting players moving into shooting positions late and often undetected.

As attacks are developed down the wings it is probable that more defenders than are necessary will move back into positions deep inside the penalty area: much nearer to goal than they need to be or goalkeepers want them to be. Crosses angled back towards the edge of the penalty area, or even headed away from goal, are likely to find other attackers unmarked if those attackers hang back on the edge of the penalty area. I mentioned earlier that attackers moving against the flow of play are unlikely to find opponents reacting to their movements, at least not instantly. The attackers, almost always, will find themselves in space and unmarked briefly.

5.5 Technical Priorities.

There are three techniques which will identify potentially outstanding skill-fulness among young, out-field, soccer players.

5.51 The ability to stop the ball: to bring it under control, with certainty.

Defenders are significantly disadvantaged when having anticipated the direction of a pass, they know that receiving players will be able to stop the ball and bring it under tight control instantly. Even worse is to know that having stopped the ball instantly, an opponent can do any of two or three different things with it.

5.52 Having controlled the ball, the ability to trick opponents with it - to dribble with it while making 'fake' moves.

Most young players kick at the ball hopefully as soon as it comes near.

The 'special' player will stop it and keep it until he decides what the most effective use of it will be. Too many young players. . . and not so young for that matter. . . let opponents influence their action options.

5.53 The skill to pass the ball or shoot in any direction,with either foot, to hit 'targets'.

The targets are three feet inside either goal post when shooting, the feet of another player or free space near enough to a teammate to allow him to move to the ball comfortably and in no immediate danger from an opponent when passing.

Exceptionally skillful players use no more than the power necessary to achieve the required result.

A shot doesn't need to be struck with maximum force; it does need to be struck accurately.

The first consideration when passing should be what sort of a pass the receiver wants and where he wants it. Poor players give passes to suit themselves or they merely get rid of the ball. . . anyhow.

Those are the three techniques upon which I would base all early development for very young players.

Without the ability to get the ball and keep it (bring it under control), all that a player can do is kick it, hopefully and anywhere.

Without control, a player can't really take part in team play.

Without the ability to trick opponents, to fool them into expecting a move in one direction or a skill used in a certain way, when a different option will be used, players are 'obvious'. Obvious players set few if any problems for their opponents.

Without the ability to pass the ball accurately where, when and how teammates need to receive it and where opponents don't, a player cannot usefully contribute to the passing and shooting aspects of the game.

To shoot effectively a player only needs to pass the ball behind an opponent (the goalkeeper) and into a goal, accurately. Some teachers teach shooting as a skill separate from passing; that's why so much of it is poor, even in professional soccer. Anyone who can pass accurately and deceptively can become a top class 'finisher' if he is prepared to shoot and to miss. . . occasionally! The great 'finishers' are those who would much rather shoot and miss than not shoot at all.

5.6 Technical Practices.

It is important to understand the differences between team, squad or group practices and those practices designed specifically for use in highly personalized teaching situations.

The former usually involve a team or squad doing similar things at the same time and under one coach or teacher. A teaching (coaching) practice is aimed specifically at one, or at a relatively small group of players.

The teacher (coach) has just the number of players he needs to enable him to develop the practice situation to suit the needs of the players and the 'activity' pattern which he has in mind. Out of a squad of players or a class, this may mean that the teacher works with four or five players, even fewer, while the rest are engaged in other work under the direction of an assistant.

5.61 Ground Control.

In diagram 31(a), the players in groups of four practice ground passing and controlling in the sequence stated.

* An unbroken line is a pass; a broken line is a player's movement without the ball.

102

Each 'end' player has a ball. A passes to B who fakes a return to A, controls the ball and turns, using the fewest possible touches, to pass to C. C passes to B who controls the ball and turns to pass to A and so on.

In diagram 31(b), A passes to B and follows his own pass.

B either returns a pass to A who dribbles on and passes to C or

B fakes a return to A but spins round and gives him the pass further on. A passes to C and runs behind him to take C's place.

C repeats the sequence from his end and it can be repeated as often as required.

* These 'end to end' or 'round' technical practices always need a

Diagram 31 (a).　　　　　　**Diagram 31 (b).**

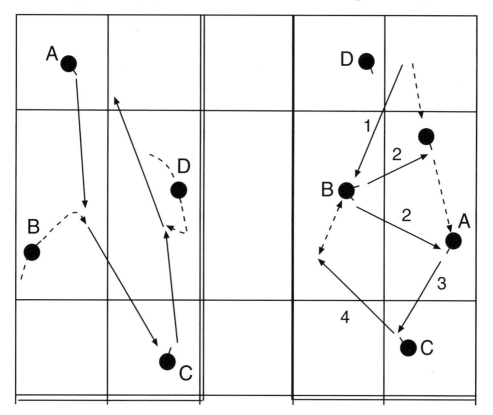

Diagram 31 (a) and (b). *End to end technical practice (ground passing).*

minimum of two players at the starting end to ensure that at least one player is always waiting to receive the final pass.

Obviously the practice described in diagram 31 can be used for any technique or combination of techniques. The only adjustment needed will be the distances between passers and receivers.

(b) Ground Control. Diagram 32.

In four groups of three, in an area 50 yds. x 40, one ball per group.

Moving freely in the practice area, players interpass in no particular sequence while avoiding contact with other players or other balls.

Progression: Three players must interpass following a set sequence e.g. A to A1 to A2, every time.

A target number of sequences is set to be achieved without contact between other players or their ball and without allowing the ball to leave the practice area.

Progression: Any player is allowed to kick another group's ball out of the practice area.

Forbidden contact or a ball kicked out of play breaks the passing sequence. The three must start again.

A progression could be to disallow any pass to a teammate's feet. All passes must be into space requiring a receiver to run onto the pass.

(c) Ground Control with a 'Fake' Move.

As previously but the receiving player must fake a controlling touch, spin away and pass. He has two touches within which to complete a pass. Possible receivers must 'read' the direction from which the pass is likely to be delivered and move accordingly.

A fake move is only successful when used sparingly and when the player's body language signals an intention quite different from the action used.

(d) Aerial Control.

The organization used for ground control can be used for practicing aerial control with or without a 'fake' move.

'Control and pass' or 'control, turn to pass' must be practiced until players can control, turn and pass in, at most, four touches for young players. Outstanding learners will quickly be down to two touches.

(e) Aerial Control with a 'Fake' Option.

Diagram 33, A serves to B using a throw or a volley kick out of hands and follows his own pass to the central position. B, moving towards the ball, 'shows' (signals) a return pass to A but turns and passes to C behind him. B follows his own pass. C throws or volleys a pass to A and follows his own

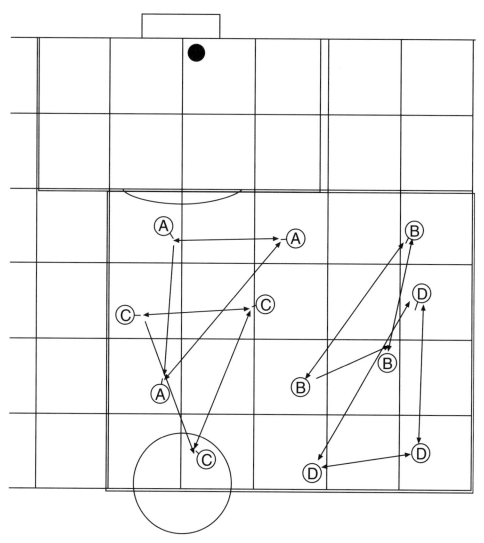

Diagram 32. *Technical practice, ground control and passing.*

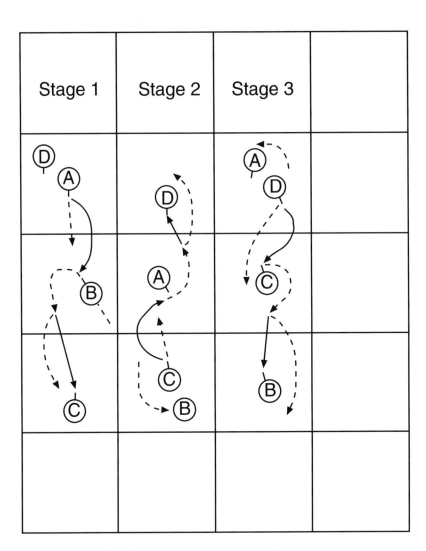

Diagram 33. *Throw/volley fake pass, control, turn and pass.*

pass.

A fakes a return pass but turns to pass to D and follows his own pass.

The sequence can be repeated without limit.

Repetitive technical practices must be carefully directed by the teacher or coach. He sets standards and introduces change (progression) when progress merits it.

It is important that players of about the same ability are in the same groups.

(f) Ground or Aerial Control and Pass Plus Fake Option. Diagram 34.
A serves to B who controls and turns to pass or fake a pass to C or D.
E can move to intercept passes only when B has made his first contact with the ball. B must pass to either C or D. When B has made his first pass, B, C, and D play 3 v 1 'keep ball' against E and try to complete a 'target' number of uninterrupted passes e.g. 10.

Progression.
As the players become more skillful, the end game becomes B, C, D against A and E. A serves and follows his serve to challenge for possession in the 3 v 2 situation.

(g) Aerial Control: conditioned game.
Area: 50 yds. x 40
Players: 10
Team organization: 3 v 3 plus 4 'floaters'.
* Floaters always play for the team with the ball.
Each team has a goalkeeper.

Attack proceeds using a fixed sequence of throw,control and pass.
The receiver of a pass ie. the third action, begins a repeat of that sequence. Goals can only be scored by headers.

A scoring attempt in the square containing the goal may be made without a controlling move ie. immediately after a throw.

(h) Aerial Control: conditioned game.
Area: 50 yds. x 40.
Players: 8 to 12.
Team organization: 4 v 4, later 4 v 1 and a goalkeeper.
The 'dead' zone (shaded) is 10 yards wide.
Two balls are in play.
A player volleys out of hands over the dead zone.

A receiving player controls the ball before it bounces and catches it or enables a teammate to catch it before it touches the ground.

The controlling player or the catcher (if different) volleys to the

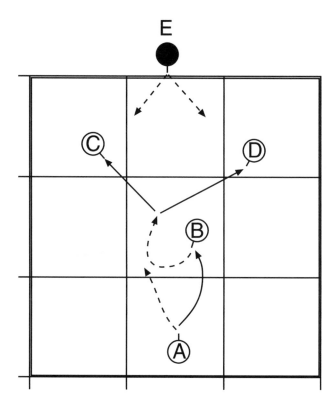

Diagram 34. *Ground or aerial control leading to 3 v 1 interpassing. The introduction of controlled opposition into technical (perceptual) practice.*

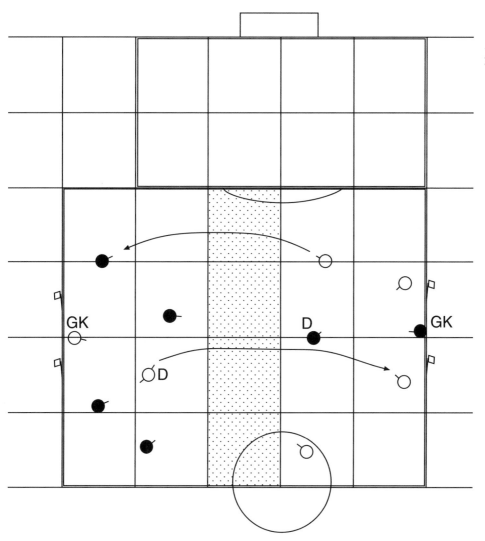

Diagram 35. *The shaded area is out of bounds.*

(1) 4 v 4. The ball is volleyed or thrown over the 'dead zone'. Receivers must control the ball in the area before returning it.

(2) At later stages, one opponent is introduced and a goal set-up. The receiving group having controlled the ball may interpass against the single opponent using a throw, control, pass sequence. Goals may be scored only following a throw, control sequence. ie. throw, control and shoot.

opponents.

Scoring: 1 point for every successful reception. 1 point deducted for every unsuccessful reception.

5.62 Dribbling And Running With The Ball.

Basically, successful dribbling requires a player to run with the ball while being able to stop, start, accelerate,decelerate or change direction to evade the challenge of an opponent or to maneuvre him off balance.

Success at the highest levels of play requires players to present 'fake' moves while dribbling; faking to stop, to start, to go this way or that, to pass or not to pass and so on.

Players being taught to dribble must be taught to 'fake' their moves at the same time. Deception when dribbling is a guarantee of success.

(a) 'Keep' Ball.

Area: 20 yds. x 20 :four 10 yard x 10 yard squares

Players: 8, four pairs.

Balls: 4

Each player in turn tries to keep the ball for a fixed time, 60 seconds say, without his opponent being able to kick it away: the ball not the player! Whenever the opponent touches the ball he scores 1 point.

Both players and the ball must remain inside the practice area all the time.

(a1.) Progression.

Each pair starts in the centre of one square. The player with the ball must try to keep the ball and move with it into any other square, 1 point: any other two squares, 3 points: or into all three other squares without being 'stopped', 5 points.

For the most skillful dribblers they may achieve all three other squares in a set order, clockwise for example.

(b) Stopping, Starting and Changing Direction

Area: 40 yds. x 20 (or the penalty area)

Players: 8 - 12

Balls: 4 - 6 (one between each pair of players)

The dribbling player tries to keep as much distance as possible between himself and his 'shadow'. On the whistle all players must stop instantly . . . or sooner!

'Shadows' try to stay within touching distance of the dribbler.

On the whistle, with both feet on the ground and without overbalancing, a shadow tries to touch his opponent.

Clever dribblers will try to keep other players between themselves and their shadows thereby becoming untouchable.

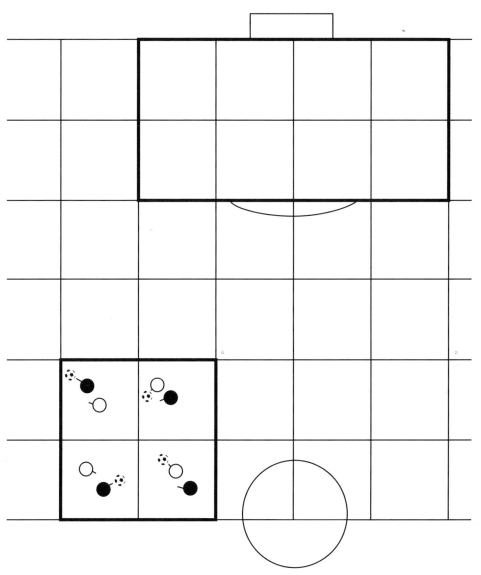

Diagram 36. *Area 20 yards x 20 yards or 20 yards x 40. 1 v 1 'keep ball' dribbling and turning to keep possession.*

(c) 'Nutmeg'.

The organization is as in (b). To 'nutmeg' an opponent in Britain is to pass the ball between his legs and run past him.

One player in each pair stands with his legs apart.

Dribblers try to pass the ball between the legs of as many stationary players as possible in a fixed time, two minutes say.

Progression.

Organization as in (c): a dribbler passes the ball past a 'stationary' player on one side while running round his other side to regain the ball. This time the stationary players keep their feet together.

A final variation involves half the stationary players having their feet apart and half together. The score is kept the same way as previously.

A further variation is that on one whistle the dribbling players must find stationary players to 'nutmeg'; on two whistles they look for players with their feet together to dribble past in the manner prescribed previously.

(d) Diagram 37. Two players,one with a ball, face each other across the line AB. The player with the ball dribbles sideways to cross the line at A or B before his opponent. Score:1 point.

Alternatively the dribbler may fake a sideways move but attack line CD instead. Score: 3 points.

The defender can only challenge when his opponent crosses line AB.

Progression.

The same organization.

A player with the ball has his back to the defending player when dribbling sideways.To attack line CD he must turn and dribble his opponent who can only challenge when the dribbler tries to cross line AB.

(e) Diagram 38.

Area: 30 yds x 30 in 10 yd. squares.

Four goals 3 yds - 5 yds. wide.

4 players start in the centre square, each attacks the goal facing them.

Score: 2 points for any goal scored and 2 extra (4 points) for dribbling past the goalkeeper to run the ball into goal. At 20 points the players change over.

(f) Using the same area, the goals are in line at the far end of the area, The attackers are faced with defenders standing 5 yards away. As attackers dribble and try to pass them, defenders cannot challenge until an attacker, with the ball, enters the final square containing the goal. The attacker can shoot or dribble to shoot and the defender can defend

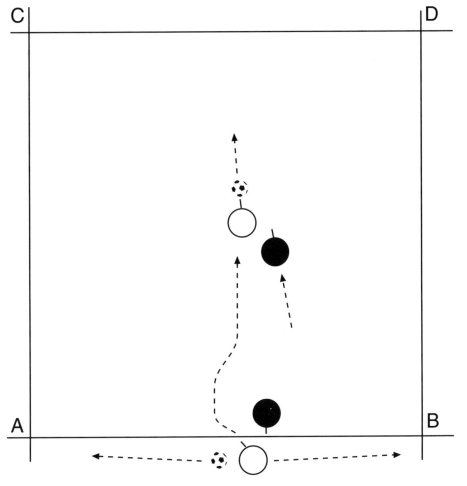

Diagram 37. *Dribbling to attack an opponent by 'moving' him sideways or by faking a sideways move and then attacking him directly.*

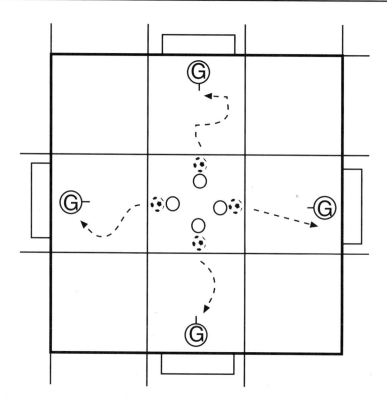

Diagram 38. *Dribble or shoot past the goalkeeper.*

positively to prevent goals being scored.
2 points per successful shot.
2 bonus points if a player dribbles through a goal.

(g) Changing Direction Late.
Area: 30 yds x 30
Goals: 2 goals at each end, 5 yards wide.
Players: 2 v 2 and one goal defender at each end.
The two black attackers, each with a ball, dribble towards the white goals. White defenders cannot challenge for the ball until the two attackers enter the mid zone (shaded). The attackers dribble through either of the two goals to score.

   The single goal defender can only defend against shots at goal or against attempts to dribble past him. Initially he cannot use his hands or arms.
Score: 1 point for a goal, two extra points for a goal scored by dribbling over a goal line.

   Where a defender dispossesses an opponent, he counter attacks and the player dispossessed must recover to defend.

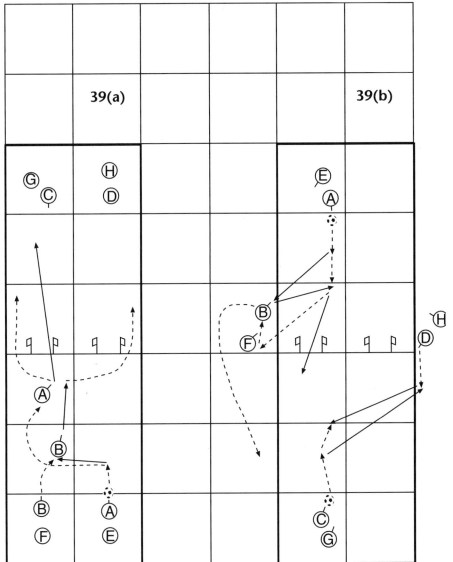

Diagram 39(a). *Pass and Shoot overlap (loop) run.*

Diagram 39(b). *Pass, return pass and shoot.*

(h) Dribbling Based Upon the Pass Option.
Area: 30 yds x 20
Goals: 5 yds wide.

Players: 2 v 2

One player must drop back to his own goal line as goal defender as soon as his side has attempted to score.

Two attackers with the ball attack the single outfield defender. Attackers score, 1 point if they interpass and move successfully behind the defender: 3 points if they fake a pass and dribble past him successfully: 1 point for a successful shot: 3 points for dribbling the ball over the goal line and between the posts.

A ball forced out of play over the side lines causes possession to be given to the other team who are immediately 2 v 1 against the other side, one of whom must drop back to his goal line.

The heavy incentive to a defender to deny wall passes or dribbling scores through the goal opens up opportunities for 'fake' wall pass moves leading to dribbling runs.

All dribbling practices should have specific 'conditions' imposed so that players are compelled or persuaded to use certain techniques.
E.g. Dribble only with the outside of the left foot (right foot). Dribble, using the sole of the foot to stop the ball. On the whistle stop the ball and pull it back with the sole of the foot before moving off in the opposite direction.

On the whistle back heel the ball and turn as quickly as possible to move off in the opposite direction to 'nutmeg' the nearest stationary player and so on.

5.63 Ground Passing and Shooting.

Deceptively skillful players can pass when they look as though dribbling may be their first option and dribble when a pass looks to be most likely. Skillful strikers can hide the direction of their shots until it is too late, almost, for a goalkeeper to do anything about it.
In fact, of course, it is never too late for a good goalkeeper!

(a) In diagram 39 (a), four pairs of players face each other at the ends of a 60 yds. x 20 practice area.
In the middle of this area are two goals, two yards wide and four yards apart. The whole makes one full width goal but the two smaller goals are the targets. A dribbles forward with the ball and passes across to B.
Having passed, A runs round behind B to receive a pass which enables him to shoot. This is an 'overlap' or a 'loop' run. A shot through the mini goals scores five points and one through the space between the mini goals, two points. Having completed a run and shot, A and B run to the opposite end

and retrieve their ball. Meanwhile C and D repeat the move from the other end and so on continuously. Occasionally B will fake a pass to A on the loop but will go on himself to shoot.

(b) Diagram 39 (b). Here there are pairs of players at each end and at the midway mark. Whatever a player's function, having completed his task he always moves 'with' the direction of the ball ie. with the practice flow.
A dribbles and passes to B outside the practice area. B gives a return pass to A enabling him to shoot first or second touch. A takes B's place in the mid area position; B moves to the far end group. C then begins the same 'dribble, pass, take a return pass from D and shoot' sequence. C takes up a position midway and D runs to the far end group.

(c) Zone Passing - Two Pairs Against The Middle Man.
Area: 30 yds. x 20
Players: Two in each end zone and one in the middle.
Balls: 1
　　The area is divided into three equal zones: passers in the end zones and one interceptor in the central zone.
　　End players pass to draw the interceptor out of position before they interpass with the pair at the other end.
　　The passing players aim for an unbroken sequence of, say, twenty passes.
If a pass is intercepted the middle man replaces the player who last played the ball.

(d) Zone Passing 2 v 1.
Area: 30 yds. x 20 later 30 yds. x 10
Players: 3
Balls: 1
　　The area is divided into three equal zones: the passing players in the end zones: the interceptor in the middle zone. The three players cannot move out of their zones.
　　The end players interpass so that the middle player cannot intercept.
Ground passes only may be used. To begin with each end player may use an unlimited number of touches before passing. Later the number of touches will be progressively reduced to a number which tests the players' controlling skill and their passing confidence. Even quite young players may reduce their touches to two.
　　For very young players it may be necessary to halve the middle zone thereby reducing the passing distance between the two end players.
　　The end players try for a pre-set target number of passes without interception as in (c) previously.

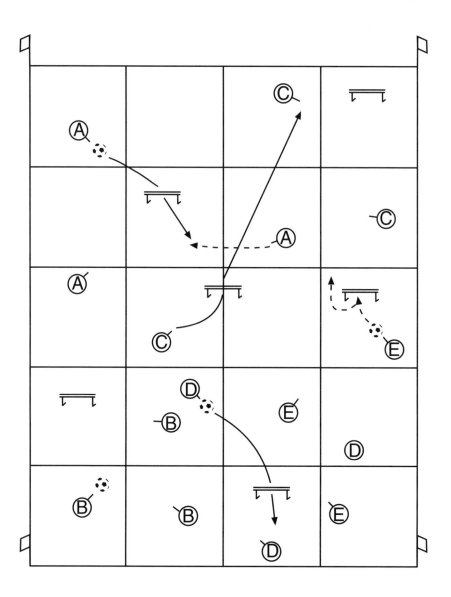

Diagram 40. *Area 50 yards x 40 containing 6 hurdles. Pairs of players interpass through the hurdles. Scoring one point each time, they are successful. Passing or receiving in the same square as a hurdle is not allowed, nor are successive passes through the same hurdle. How many passes can be made in 2 minutes?*

(e) Diagram 40.
Area: 50 yds x 40 or less.
Players: 12 -18 in pairs or threes
Hurdles: 6
Balls: one to each group of two or three.
The groups interpass to pass the ball through as many hurdles as possible in a set time: two minutes say.

Two or more players from the same group cannot occupy the same square. The ball cannot pass through the same hurdle twice in succession. While trying to score themselves, one group can stop others' passes scoring through hurdles; they can kick other groups' balls out of play to deny them time to pass and score.

To position himself effectively a player must be constantly aware of other players, both opponents and likely 'target' players.

Visualizing a teammate's passing 'line' between two opponents and moving to receive it, diagram 40, a vitally important, perceptual skill; the success of 'through' passes depends on it. Through passes are absolutely fundamental to achieving attacking penetration. Passing the ball into space for other attackers to move onto, often unnoticed and clear of defenders, is part of the game's artistry.

(f) Diagram 41.
Area: 40 yds. x 30
Goals: 6, each 3 yds wide
Players: 2 v 2 or 3 v 3 and 1 Floater.
Initially, interpassing may lead to a 'passing shot' from anywhere in the area. As skill improves, 'passing shots' may be taken only from the two central zones, ie. at least ten yards away from goals.

With skilled players 'shots' may be restricted to the back two zones ie. from a team's own half of the area.

This game can be adapted to focus teaching and practice emphasis on different skills.

(g) Organization as above.
In addition to the 2 v 2 plus 1 floater, each team has an additional attacker who operates only in the front zone. Diagram 41.

To score, the ball must be played to a 'front player' who passes back to the oncoming player to shoot quickly and accurately.

Only the 'front' players may occupy their zones which they may not leave.

Passing backwards to move forwards is an important tactical skill and not only in Ireland!

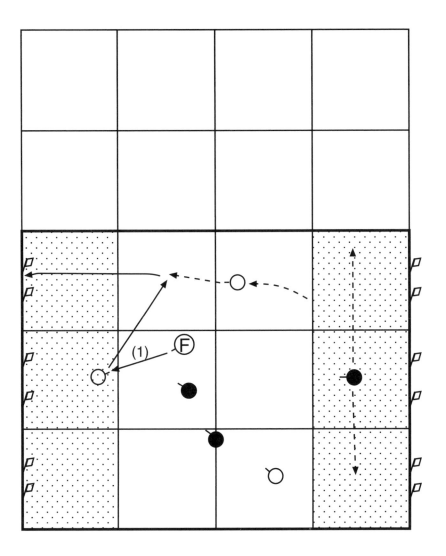

Diagram 41. *3 v 3 and floater. Passing into front attackers and moving to shoot from 'pass backs'.*

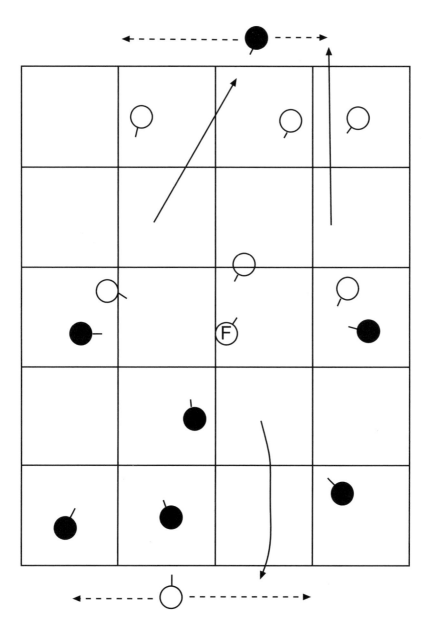

Diagram 42. *F and 3 v 3 passing to play 'through' passes to end players.*

(h) Switching the direction of attack to give through passes.
Area: 50 yds. x 40.
Players: 3 v 3 plus 1 floater in the central zone.

3 defenders in each end zone
1 pass receiver behind each end zone.

Players starting in a particular zone are confined there. The 'floater' always plays with the team in possession of the ball. Central zone players try to score by passing the ball between end zone defenders to the pass receivers.

In all practices, whether perceptive, preceptive or even conceptive in format, players should be encouraged to create fantasy soccer situations in their minds. Everything they do in practice should be imagined as occurrences in the real game; this is particularly true for perceptual practice, what some might describe as routine, technical practice. Nothing should ever be allowed to become routine. Occasionally, players should be encouraged to do something different to the practice theme to ensure that whatever they are doing, they are thinking soccer.

Aerial Passing and Shooting.
(a) In diagram 43, the players AD and CB pass over the mid-zone.
A passes over the mid-zone to to B who controls the ball and passes to C.C passes over the mid-zone to D and the rotation is repeated and regularly reversed, clockwise to anti-clockwise and so on.

(b) As in diagram 43 previously, but now a goal has been placed on the central mid-zone line. The goal has two smaller goals, each two yards wide within it. The passing sequence is repeated but this time, having received a short pass from B for example, C shoots to score.

If he scores through either of the mini goals he gains four points: through the central goal area he gains two.

With skillful players a goalkeeper may be introduced later. Initially he must save without using his hands or arms.

(c) In diagram 44, two players patrol the central square. They may intercept the ball using any part of their bodies to do so EXCEPT hands or arms.

Later, dependent on the skill of the players in adjusting the degrees of height on their passes, they may use their hands or arms.

(d) Diagram 44. In an area 40 yds x 60, the central zone is patrolled by two players who can intercept passes using any part of the body except hands or arms.

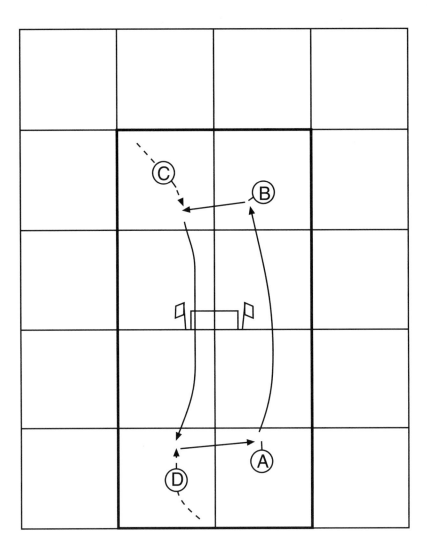

Diagram 43. *Lofted pass, aerial control and 'set-up' for shots at goal.*

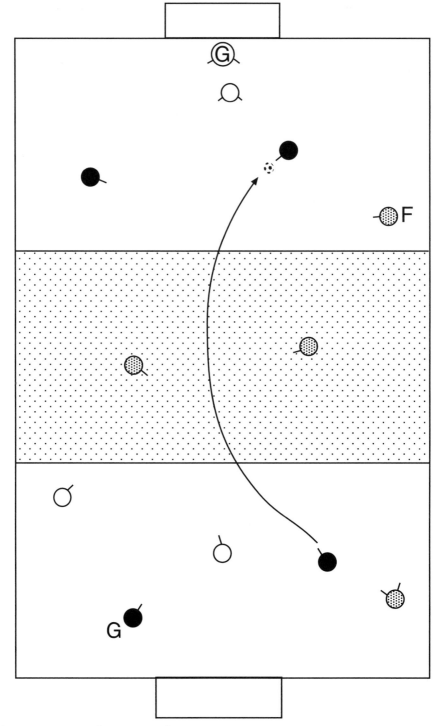

Diagram 44. *Aerial Passing and Receiving.*

In the two end zones, each 40 yards x 20, there are three attackers opposed by one defender. They interpass until one can loft a pass over the mid-zone to the three players at the other end. They also play 3 v 1 until they can repeat the pass over the mid-zone to the opposite end. If the ball is intercepted in an end zone or on its way over the mid-zone the interceptors change with those who allowed the ball to be intercepted. Score according to the number of completed aerial passes in unbroken sequence.

(e) In diagram 44, goals have been erected at each end. The ball is put into play by being lofted over the mid-zone.

At each end there are two 'teams' of two with one 'floater. The floater always joins the side which has the ball.

When an attack has been completed the floater joins the team trying to pass, now 3 v 2, to the other end.

First receivers of long passes must attempt to control the ball in the air before interpassing to shoot. The goalkeeper must remain on his goal line until an attacker enters the end zone in front of goal.

(f)
Area: 40 yds. x 30 with a goal zone at each end, 30 yds. x 10.
Players: 2 v 2 with 2 floaters who are always with the attacking team.
Balls: 1
Goals: 2 x 5 yds wide goals at each end.
Players attack using a 'throw, control (in the air), pass' sequence to make progress end to end. When in an end zone, the sequence may become 'throw, control, pass and shoot'. Initially there are no goalkeepers: later they may be introduced.

5.64 Long Passing With Swerve.
Players should learn to understand the cause and effect of swerve from early ages. They add dimensions of expression to players' fundamental skills which are exciting to experiment with and not least because the higher a player's ambitions in soccer, the greater his need for extraordinary techniques in play. Obvious players are, well. . . obvious!

(a) Principles.
Imagine the surface of a ball in front of you to be marked with a cross.
(1)   If the ball is struck anywhere along the vertical line and below the horizontal line the ball will rise.

(2)   The nearer to the ground that it is struck the greater the angle of 'lift' and the greater the back spin effect imparted to the ball. In

normal ground conditions, on hitting the ground back spin will resist forward movement and the ball will 'hold' rather than run on.

(3) The nearer to the horizontal mid-line the ball is struck, the less the angle of lift and the less the back spin effect. The ball will travel straight and, in normal ground conditions, will continue to travel on after hitting the ground.

(4) If the ball is struck below the horizontal mid-line and to the right of the vertical mid-line, area A, the ball will lift, and swerve in the air from right to left. Swerve comes from the right to left diagonal spin imparted by the kick.

Given sufficient spin, when the ball hits the ground it will 'break' from left to right.

The opposite is true if the ball is struck in area B. The ball will lift and swerve left to right and 'break' from right to left.

(5) If the ball is struck through the horizontal mid-line the ball will stay on the ground; if it is struck slightly above the mid line the ball will stay on the ground and forward (top) spin will be imparted.

(6) Striking the ball as in (4) and to one side or the other will cause the ball to swerve along the ground and in a direction opposite to the side of the ball which has been kicked.

On a pitch with a good carpet of grass, swerve will be possible but not as great as in the air. The length of grass resists both spin (and consequently swerve) and forward travel.

Understanding the cause and effect of spin and swerve is important for all players, especially for goalkeepers. Spin and swerve are used to cause goalkeeper misjudgments. Goalkeepers rarely have had the experience of imparting and reading spin and swerve which should have been part of an outfield player's upbringing from a very early age. Even so I have seen senior out-field players who were poor 'readers' of off-the-ground 'break' caused by spinning the ball.

Black and white 'spotted' soccer balls assist in developing this understanding; players can see the spin and swerve effects and can relate them almost instantly to kicking method. This is 'feed back' of results at its very best.

(7) The same swerve and spin can be imparted using the outside of one foot or the inside of the other: teach and encourage practice with both. One footed players place themselves and their teams at a serious disadvantage sooner or, usually, later.

(b) Practices.

(1) In diagram 45, player A from the centre line swerves a pass over the mid zone to B. B controls the ball in the air or on the ground and plays a short pass to C in the central zone. C gives a return ground pass to B who hits a swerved pass to A. C now moves to receive a short pass from A to whom he returns the ball and the sequence is repeated.

As the players' swerve kicking improves, the kicking player and the target player move to extreme wide positions from which to deliver and receive the passes.

It is much easier to hit swerved passes when the ball is moving towards the player who will strike it. Also it is easier to control swerve against the wind rather than with it.

(2) In diagram 46, there are three marks five yards apart on each side of the penalty area. Starting on the mark furthest from the goal line, players try to swerve the ball directly into goal without touching the ground in between. As they improve they kick the ball from the next mark towards the goal line.

Eventually they aim to swerve kick into goal from the goal line. Very skillful 'swervers' may kick directly into goal from marks along the goal line and out towards the corner flag. A left footed kick from the left side of the goal will be hit with the outside of the left foot. From the right side, a left footed kick will be hit with the inside of the left foot.

(3) In diagram 47, the practice area is 40 yds x 30, divided into three long zones. Four players are in each of the zones and two balls are in play.

The outside teams try to swerve a target number of kicks over the mid-zone without interception.

Players are 'conditioned' to use a specific surface of the kicking foot, e.g. the outside. Failure to do so loses the team three points. If a pass fails to clear the mid zone the offending player loses one point for his team. The passing teams score one point for every successful swerve kick across the zone. Both passing teams aim to reach twenty points first. The team which loses changes place with the four mid-zone players.

(4) Within the practice area 40 yds x 30 there is a 'no go' zone occupied by 2 interceptors. The 4 players outside the central zone, one to each side of the area, pass the ball over the interceptors to build up an unbroken

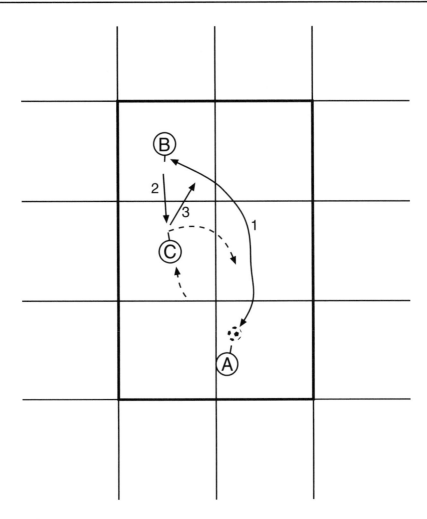

Diagram 45. *Swerving aerial passes using the outside of one foot or the inside of the other foot.*

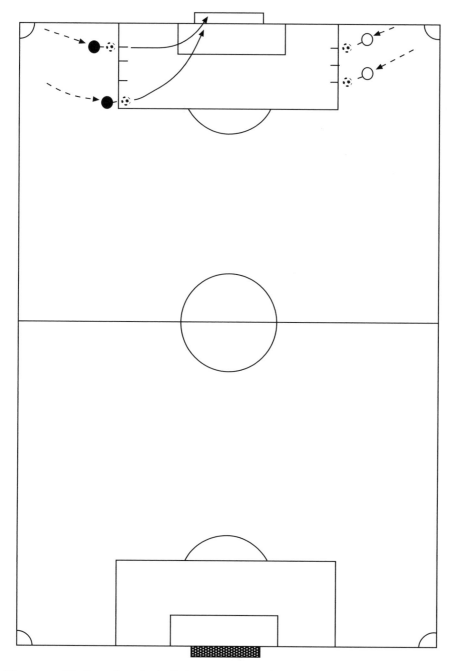

Diagram 46. *Swerving the ball directly into goal using both sides of the feet.*

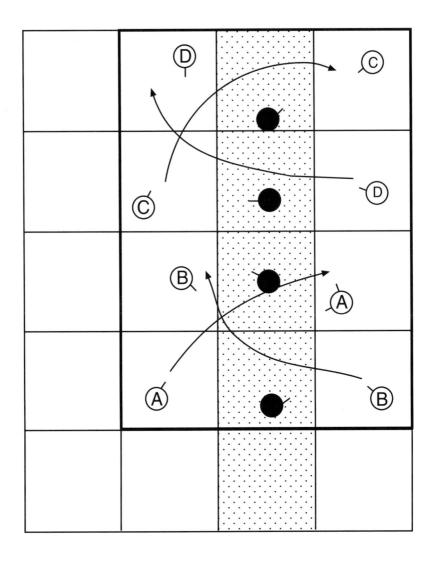

Diagram 47. *Swerve passing across an interceptors' zone using different surfaces of both feet.*

sequence of passes. If the ball passes outside the full area or fails to clear the central zone, costs the '4' group two points.

Ground passes may be made directly across the central zone from one side to an opposite side only and they score no points. They may help a receiver to swerve a subsequent pass. A successful, swerved pass scores 5 points. A '4' group is allowed 20 contacts to make as high a score as possible. The two interceptors must remain within the central zone and initially may not use hands or arms to intercept passes.

(5) In diagram 48, the practice area is 40 yds x 40 yds. The goalkeeper is not allowed inside the semi circular area six yards from goal. There are two wide players on each side and they are confined, unopposed, to their corner squares. In mid field the contest is 2 v 2 with 1 floater who plays for whichever side has the ball. All players can score. A goal shot from a corner area scores 5 points.

A goal scored from any part of mid field scores 1 point.

5.54 Heading.
(a) Principles.
(1) Successful and painless heading, the same thing really, comes from striking the ball with the flat frontal surface of the forehead. The results of heading with other surfaces may be painful, which we can tolerate, and inaccurate, which we can't.

(2) The head should be turned so that the ball is always directed off the front forehead.

(3) However hard the ball is struck, a player should move to hit the ball with his forehead rather than allow the ball to hit him.

(4) For headed strikes on goal and most passes the ball is nodded downwards. Effective, headed clearances are achieved by throwing the forehead at the underneath part of the ball, lifting it upwards and outwards for optimum distance.

(b) Practices.
(1) Early practice aims at creating confidence in making contact between ball and head painlessly and accurately and in that order.

Any practice using a 'throw, head, catch' or 'throw, head, control' sequence involving a thrown service to a player required to head in a certain way will do to begin with. Nervous players should be encouraged to throw for themselves.

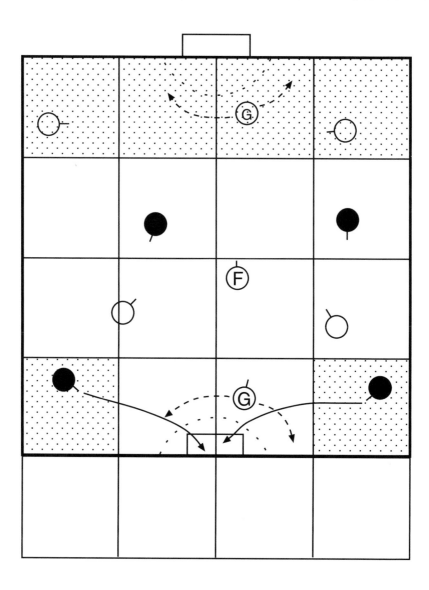

Diagram 48. *5 v 5 and 1 floater. Swerve shooting.*

In pairs, self serving players may practice heading to a partner or at a target two or three yards away. The distance is increased as players learn to move their bodies forward into the forward 'throwing' action of forehead to ball. Targets might be a partner's hands held at different levels from ground to full stretch over head. Practice starts with both players standing still, later the target player will move to test the heading player's ability to change direction of headers.

Heading for distance contests are useful early practices.

(2) In threes, players practice throw, head, catch sequences. A throws to B who heads the ball to be caught by C.

A major block to progress can occur when another player throws the ball for a partner to head. Mental 'blocks' occur at this stage and also when thrown services are changed to kicks. The force generated in any service must be controlled so that the player never loses confidence through the fear of a painful consequence of heading.

The receiving player in a group of three should move from almost in front of the heading player to a position at right angles to him.

Heading players should learn, early, to turn their heads to direct the ball, not to flick at it with the side of the head.

(3) In threes, players keep the ball in the air to achieve the largest number of headers in an unbroken sequence.

(4) In diagram 49, 12 players, in threes, can move anywhere in the

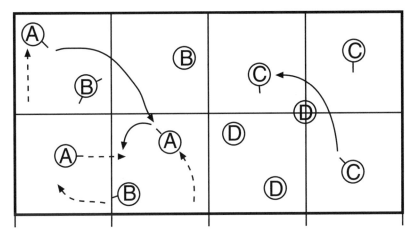

Diagram 49. *Throw, head, catch on the run inside the penalty area.*

penalty area or in an area 40 yds x 20. Each player to receive a throw must have a player from another group of three between himself and the thrower. The 'threes' practice the throw, head, catch (or control) sequence while running from one end of the area to the other. The ball must never touch the ground. Later the sequence becomes throw, head, control and pass using a soccer technique to control and then pass.

(5) 3 v 1 or 4 v 1 depending upon the heading skill of the players. The area is 40 yds x 20 for 3 v 1 and 50 x 20 for 4 v 1. Each player heading the ball, having had it thrown to him, can head to any of his teammates. If downward heading is to be practiced, the sequence becomes throw, head downwards, control and set up an inter-passing sequence of, say, three or four consecutive passes.

The purpose of practice is to expose players to increasingly realistic situations in which soccer judgment is involved to an increasing extent.

(6) Players are then introduced to jumping to head the ball. A and B stand still about three yards apart. C serves under arm above the gap between A and B. D runs forward to jump to head the ball back to C. The service from C must always be far enough away from D to enable him to make some sort of adjustment in his run up to take off.

As the players' confidences increase the standing players move fractionally closer together but they do not interfere with the player jumping to head. The gap between A and B decreases until D must brush through and past them to jump to head.

Almost any 'block' to learning the skill of jump heading is fear of the presence of other players, collision with whom might cause injury. This is similarly true of goalkeepers jumping to catch or punch high balls.

(7) The area is 60 yards x 20 with two goals. 2 play against 2 with 4 players who are 'floaters' (floaters always play for the side which has possession of the ball which effectively produces a 6 v 2 situation).

In attack, one player kicks (or throws) the ball out of hand to a second player who heads to any third player; the third player catches the ball and sets up the same sequence: kick, head, catch. A goal may be attempted only in the end zones and is scored when a player receiving a kicked or thrown pass heads into goal. No one may handle the ball to prevent a scoring header. The number of players can vary but with young players at early stages of heading development, the number of floaters should always ensure that the attacking team heavily outnumbers the defenders.

(8) To head the ball away from goal is a frequently needed defensive skill. It must be done safely and accurately. If there are risks, the defender should try to head the ball as far away from goal as he can. He tries to gain time (distance) for other defenders to move the primary defensive barrier as far from goal as possible and to generally reorganize. Heading for distance means that optimum force is needed to lift it upwards and outwards. It involves precisely the same principles as kicking for distance. The only difference is that for the former the ball presents little inertia to overcome since it is in the air and moving at impact.

In threes, A heads over C to B. Initially C stands still; later he can jump to intercept or block the header.

Progression. C throws to A who heads over him to B.

Progression. B, on the opposite side of C, throws to A who heads back to him over C's attempted interception.

(9) 2 players stand on each side of a goal and within an area 8 yds x 8. A throws to B who heads over the goal to the opponents C and D. C or D control the ball and then catch it before it touches the ground. The sequence of throw head, control and catch is repeated end to end.

Points are scored for successful headers and lost for those which fall to the ground.

Progression. A receiving player must control the ball and then play a short volley or header to his partner.

(10) **In diagram 50**, the area is 40 yds x 20 approximately a normal penalty area. The black players other than the goalkeeper remain still. A throws or gives a short volley into the shaded area. Attackers B and C run to jump and head for goal. Later the services will be aimed above the heads of the black players: attackers must jump to head for goal over and above them.

5.55 Tackling.
(a) Principles
Fair and harmless tackling requires care, judgment and timing: a great

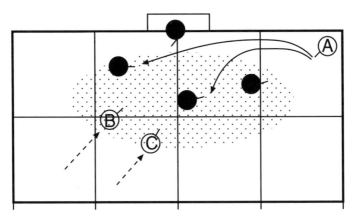

Diagram 50. *Turning in to jump above defenders to head for goal.*

deal of it isn't. Of all soccer's skills, tackling is the one least likely to be taught, coached or practiced.

(1) To block the ball when dribbled or kicked by an opponent the largest surface of the foot is planted firmly behind the ball just as the opponent contacts the ball; not after and certainly not before.

(2) The full weight of the body is held behind the blocking foot having been moved into that position as the tackle is made.

If the weight of the tackling player is over or slightly in front of the tackling foot he can only resist his opponent with his leg, mostly from the knee down. This is a dangerous and weak position for the knee joint complex. Ligaments are strained or ruptured in this way.

Having blocked the ball in the tackle, possession is won by the player able to force the ball away from or over the foot of his opponent.

(3) Effective tacklers wait until an opponent moves his foot to play the ball, then they strike.

To lift one foot off the ground to play the ball, a player must transfer his weight onto his standing foot. Momentarily he cannot have his full weight behind the ball when tackled.

(b) Practices.
Early teaching will concentrate on the timing of the move into a tackling position. Both players must try to time their strikes for the ball simultaneously. Achievement will increase players' confidence and tackling, of all soccer's skills, is a matter of confidence.

One player arriving early or late into the tackle and someone is likely to be hurt.

(1) Two players stand well balanced in the tackling position with their feet firmly wedged behind the ball. Each tries to force the ball away from his opponent.

Progression:
(2) Each player takes one stride back from the ball and strikes for the tackling position from there.

(3) The players walk into the tackle from about three steps away. Each times his approach so that they strike for the ball at exactly the same moment.

(4) In an area 20 yds x 10, two players face each other and the ball on the mid-line and three or four strides from it. On each end line there is a goal five yards wide. On a signal, the players walk forward into a tackle. Theplayer who succeeds in winning possession of the ball is allowed to move the ball forward two steps before placing the ball down. The walk into the tackle procedure is repeated.

Whichever player wins a tackle moves the ball two steps towards his opponent's goal. Tackling to gain ground carries on until the ball arrives at a mark five yards from goal. Here the winning player takes a penalty kick. The game is restarted from the central position.

(5) **In diagram 51,** 8 players are in an area 20 yds x 20. Along each side there are gates, each of which is 5 yards wide. 4 players have a ball each. They dribble the ball anywhere in the area trying to dribble through gates as many times as possible in a set time. They try to avoid tackles, or if tackles are made, struggle to keep possession of the ball. When possession is lost, the successful tackler carries on dribbling and resisting or evading tackles for as long as he can. Each time the ball is dribbled through one of the gates a point is scored.

Players without the ball tackle to gain possession to score and to prevent other players from scoring. Kicking the ball out of the practice area doesn't count as a successful tackle.

(6) **In diagram 52,** the area is 40 yds x 20 divided into 10 yard zones. Players with the balls start on the first line, their opponents five paces behind. On the signal, players with the balls try to dribble as far up the course as they can while their opponents race to overtake them and

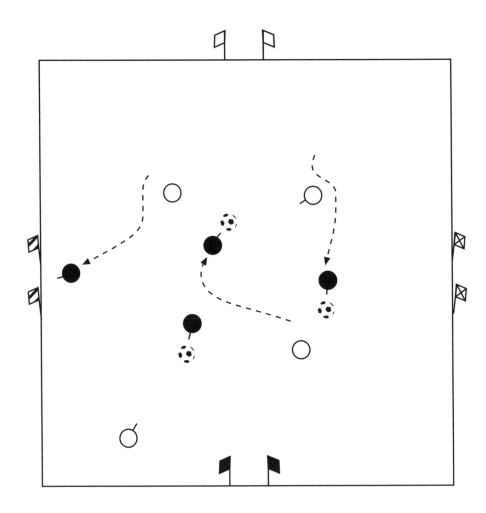

Diagram 51. *Dribbling and Tackling.*

tackle for the ball from the side and front. A player with a ball is not allowed to turn back to avoid a tackle.

The lines are numbered 1 to 3; a player scores according to the line over which he has dribbled without losing the ball.

The side block tackle is needed when a pursuing player reaches a position at least level with a dribbling player, preferably slightly in front of him. In that position the tackler can pivot on his inside foot and turn into a similar position adopted for the front block tackle. The further behind the tackler is the less the chance he has for turning into the blocking position with his weight behind his tackling foot.

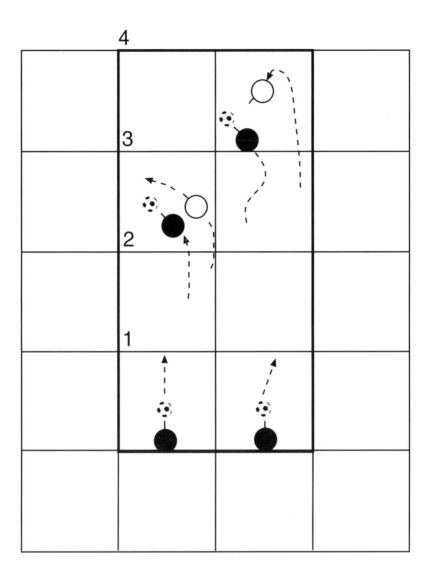

Diagram 52. *Dribbling up the ladder to resist tackles.*

(7) **Diagram 53.** An area 30 yds x 60 is divided into three equal zones. In each of the end zones there is one attacker with two defenders. At one end there is an orthodox goal: at the other two small goals. In the mid zone there are two players from each team.

Players must remain in the zone in which they start the practice. There are no goalkeepers as such but any single defender may act as a goal-keeper should the need arise. In the end zones, one defender must mark his opponent. The ball must be passed forward through each zone or backwards and forwards through each zone.

One against two in the attacking zones means that the attacker must dribble to try to score which gives opponents unlimited opportunities for practicing tackling.

(8) **In diagram 54,** the area is 40 yds x 40 (approximately two penalty areas). In each half there are three defenders and two attackers and no goalkeepers so that two defenders are able to man mark the two attackers. This compels attackers to hold the ball and dribble since passing opportunities will be limited; the defenders have increased opportunities for tackling and for intercepting practice.

The attacking players lose one point if they accept a pass and keep their bodies between a defender and the ball for longer than a three second count. They must make every attempt to receive and turn to dribble (or pass) to defeat their opponents.

When running alongside a player dribbling the ball, a side block tackle is most safely made when the player with the ball is using the foot nearer to the tackler to play it forward. If the dribbler transfers the ball to the far side foot a block tackle is impossible and if attempted dangerous. . . to the tackler.

In those circumstances a tackler can only slide across his opponent and try to knock the ball away and preferably out of play. To try to slide across a dribbling opponent using the foot and leg nearer to him is, once again, very dangerous for the tackling player. A slide tackle often brings down the dribbler: it shouldn't but it does!

A player falling across an out-stretched leg which itself is off the ground and unsupported results often in very serious injuries to the ligaments of the knee. Don't do it!

Slide tackling should not be taught as part of a young player's repertoire of techniques.

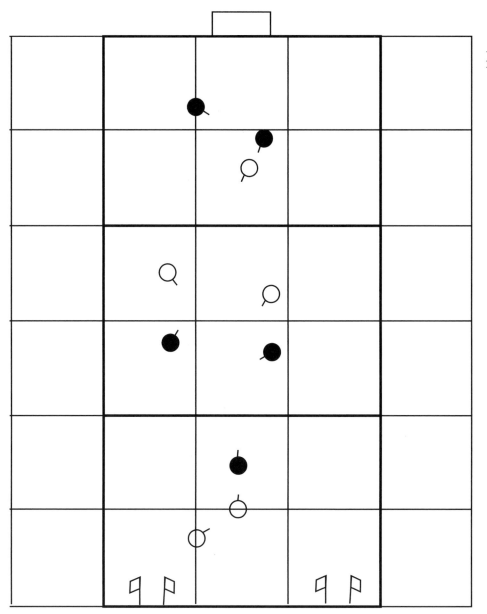

Diagram 53. *1 v 2 dribbling and tackling practices always play through the zones.*

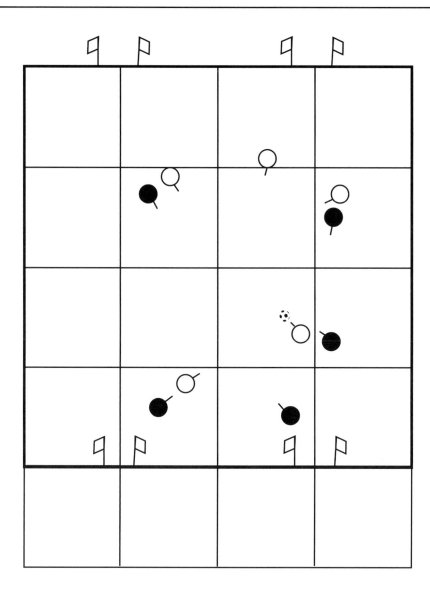

Diagram 54. *2 v 3. Dribbling, passing intercepting and tackling.*

5.56 Intercepting.

The ability to 'read' what is happening in a game and thereby to work out what is likely to happen is a very important skill. Without learning to 'read' play (and players), intercepting passes between opponents becomes a matter of chance rather than skill.

Pass interceptions give a player an enormous attacking advantage. Intercepting, in my view, is more important than tackling but both have their place in the game. Players who do neither place their teams at serious disadvantages.

(a) Principles.

Learning to 'read' another player involves:

(1) Knowing which foot he mostly (or always) uses. That will tell an interceptor which foot he may take risks with. A player forced to pass with his weaker foot will take more time to do so and will concentrate more on making the required accuracy of contact with the ball. If he's concentrating on the ball he can't concentrate on a possible interceptor. . . at least not enough to prevent that player beginning his move to intercept early.

(2) Watching other players' eyes without being caught doing it. Even high class players have to look to assess what they may need to do. Assessment takes time; time makes their intentions more predictable. The greater the degree of predictability, the better the odds in favor of an interception.

(3) Judging a player's quality of 'touch'. Players may have a good range of techniques: these can be revealed within a few minutes' play. What is more important to anyone looking for interceptions is the degree to which a player can guarantee speed, accuracy and a high degree of sensitivity in what he does. A player may be able to control the ball with almost every part of his body but if that control usually allows the ball to bounce two or three feet away, interceptions are always going to be possible.

A passing player may be highly accurate but if he delivers a pass with so much weight that the receiving player has controlling difficulties then again interceptions are always going to be possible, certainly worth risking.

(4) There are two sources of signals which enable a defender to intercept passes successfully, the first come from the passing player. He looks for his target player and sets himself to make the delivery. Setting himself means that he concentrates on making the required contact with the ball.

An interceptor must watch for these signals.

He should also look for any unusual alertness in the general behavior of any potential pass receiver. Most players worth the name sense when their teammates are likely to give a pass, it is part of the experience gained from playing regularly with other players. Alertness comes when a player intends to move quickly in order to be in the best position to receive and use a pass when it arrives.

'Naturalists' would have us believe that players are born with these 'senses'; that is nonsense; they are learned and in good soccer schools they are taught.

(5) Having assessed the probability of a pass, the interceptor will watch for the passing player dropping his eyes to concentrate on hitting the ball accurately. That is the time to move closer to the target player preparing to intercept the pass when it is given.

(b) Practices.
(1) In an area 20 yds x 10, 2 players inter-pass against 1. The passing players are allowed two touches only, one to control and one to pass which with young players should present plenty of opportunities for making interceptions.

As intercepting skill improves, the situation may be increased to 3 v 1. Initially the players will have their 'touches' limited to one or two, giving the interceptor reasonable chances of intercepting passes.

(2) In the same area, the width is 30 yds and the length only 10 yds. Diagram 55. A goal 10 yds wide is in the middle of each end line. Two inter-pass against 2 trying to run the ball through the goal to score. They are each allowed a limited number of touches: the fewer the number, the easier the interceptions. When the interceptor wins the ball he tries to run it through the goal at the other end.

Interceptions enable an intercepting player to move quickly into counter attack if he thinks quickly enough.

(2) Diagram 56.
Area: 40 yds x 30.
Goals: 4, each 5 yds wide. 2 for each team.
Players: 3 pairs and two feeders (F) on each side.

The feeders only serve passes into the receivers, they are not

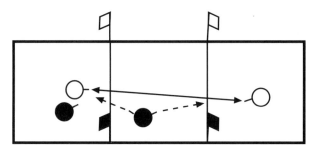

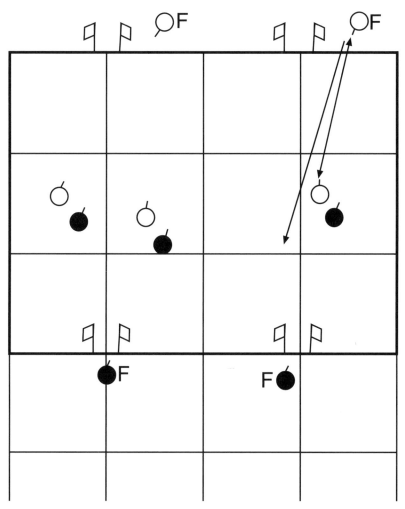

Diagram 55. *Intercepting.*

Diagram 56. *Feeders, receivers and interception.*

goalkeepers. The feeders, behind the goal lines, can receive return passes from the in-field players. On pitch receivers try to turn with the ball to run it through one of the two goals behind them. Score 2 points. Marking players try to intercept passes to run the ball through either of the goals facing them. Score 4 points.

Later and having made an interception, the interceptor must also turn and attack the goal behind him. He is now the pass receiver and the original receiver becomes the interceptor. Feeders will not only look for passes to the feet of receivers they will also look for chances to pass behind both receivers and interceptors thereby allowing receivers to spin quickly to collect what are in effect through passes.

If, having turned, a receiver is then successfully stopped from scoring, the tackler scores 2 points.

Feeders, receivers and interceptors rotate their respective functions.

(3) Diagram 57.

Area: 60 yds x 30
Goals: 6, each 5 yds wide. 3 to each team.
Players: 4 pairs and 1 sweeper (free defender) at each end.

Each team's sweeper has possession in turn. He passes to one of his four players who inter-pass to try to defeat the marking and intercepting attempts of their opponents. Score 5 points for every goal scored by running the ball over the line and into one of the three goals.

The sweeper cannot move forward and cannot be tackled or challenged. Whenever he receives the ball his touches are limited. He can receive passes from central zone players and he can play to feet or into space.

The shape of the area encourages sideways play giving defenders ample opportunities for practicing intercepting.

(4) Diagram 58.

Area: 60 yds x 20.
Players: two in each zone and one behind each end line.

The ball is put into play from behind the end line. The players in the first area struggle for possession. Whichever player wins the ball passes to his teammate in the next area 'up the ladder'. The ball may be passed back one area before being played forward again but no more than three times after which possession is given to the other team.

Each team tries to claim the larger number of possessions in climbing the ladder.

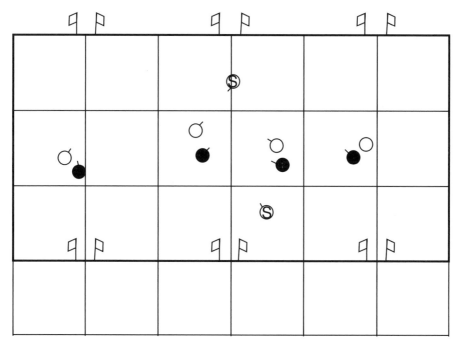

Diagram 57. *4 pairs and sweepers marking and intercepting practice sweepers are 'protected.'*

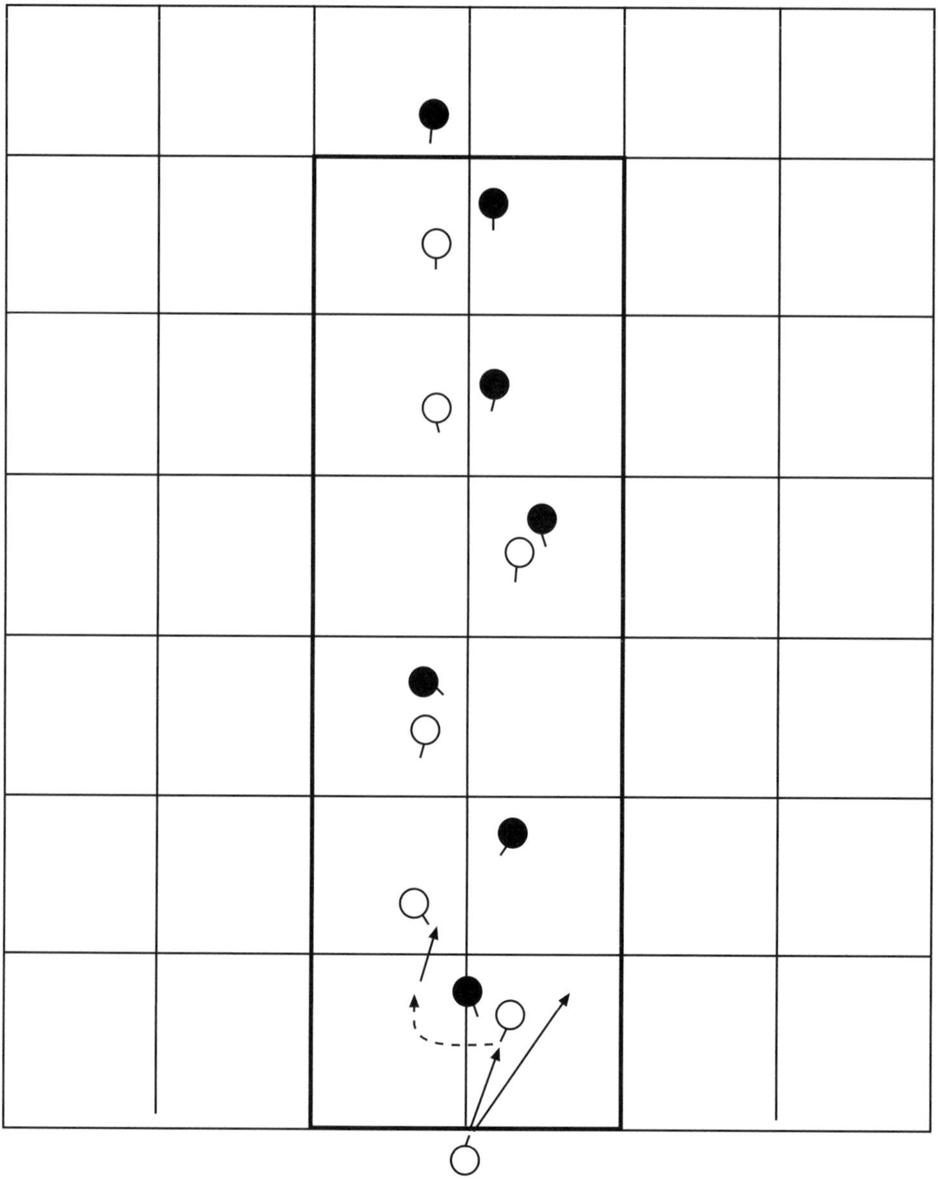

Diagram 58. *Passing and intercepting on the ladder.*

(5)
Area: 40 yds x 60 marked out in three zones each 20 yds deep.
Players: 2 v 1 in each end zone and 2 v 2 in the middle zone.

Starting at one end a team tries to work the ball through each zone in turn. The final receiver is alone against two opponents. If he succeeds in receiving the ball, he may try to reverse the movement back to the other end and if successful his team scores 4 points and a four point bonus.

A team which moves the ball successfully from one end to the other scores 2 points.

If the defending team stops the move but doesn't reverse it, the ball is put into play from their end.

(6) In general play: 6 v 6 on an area 60 yds x 40, award two points for a goal and four points to any player intercepting. A large incentive for interceptions enhances the practice objective.

Interceptions attempted unrealistically present the teacher with opportunities to teach.

Practice 'conditions', carefully selected and applied, make skill practice so much more relevant to the skill needed in the full game.

To produce tackling opportunities for example, teams must be given incentives to dribble; without dribbling, tackling opportunities are limited.

To produce intercepting possibilities, teams must be given incentives to pass, especially across the field.

The design of effective practices requires a teacher or coach to think laterally. 'Lateral thinking' approaches a problem from an unusual angle, often the opposite to the most obvious approach.

5.57 Charging An Opponent.
Not many, if any, soccer teaching or coaching books deal with this important aspect of the game. Soccer permits fair body contact but not violent play; the difference is clear but follows a fine line.

Violence is the excessive use of force and is likely to be dangerous to one or both players involved.

(a) Principles.
(1) A player may charge an opponent, shoulder to shoulder, when both players are trying to play the ball.

(2) He may charge an opponent from behind, even in the back, when that opponent is using obstruction to prevent him from playing the ball.

(3) He may also charge a goalkeeper who is obstructing him from playing the ball.

Outside the penalty area of course the goalkeeper is subject to the laws in the same way as any other player.

The secret of effective and fair charging is to wait until the opponent is moving his weight onto his outside foot, the foot furthest away from the challenging player.

A runner must move his weight, side to side, in order that he can lift each foot off the ground and swing it forward into stride.

A shoulder to shoulder charge, as the player moves off his near foot onto the foot further from the charging player, propels him in the direction of his weight transference and therefore off balance.

Where two players are set to charge each other, it may pay one of them to 'fake' a charge and at the last moment to pull away from it leaving the opponent committed and likely to lose his balance.

(b) Practices.

(1) Player B walks alongside player A who dribbles the ball; B may challenge for the ball shoulder to shoulder. Whichever player wins the challenge sprints away with the ball for the line ten to twenty yards in front. The losing player recovers to challenge and tackle.

When the players have mastered the timing of the challenge at walking pace, they repeat the practice at jogging pace: both moving in the same direction.

At this early stage it is useful if each pair is about the same height. Tall players must bend if they are to achieve shoulder to shoulder and therefore fair contact.

(2) Area: 40 yds x 20 (or the penalty area)

10 - 15 players dribble a ball each anywhere in the area. Five 'hunters' can move anywhere to challenge for possession by shoulder charging a dribbling player. The ball can only be kicked away by a challenger after he has made a shoulder to shoulder challenge. Whichever player wins the challenge carries on as the ball dribbler. The former dribbler now becomes a hunter looking for someone to charge for possession.

(3) The players face each other in pairs about five yards apart.

On a signal the players walk towards each other, one with the ball. As they close, they turn their shoulders towards each other to charge for possession at the same time as they tackle. The practice is repeated at jogging pace and if successful in winning the ball a player tries to dribble the ball to a line ten yards behind.

(4) Two players stand shoulder to shoulder across a line. On a signal they shoulder charge each other to try to gain enough space to enable one

or the other to cross the line into his opponent's territory.

(5) Two players A and B face a third player C who has the ball. C
passes the ball towards A and B and between them. A and B charge
and challenge for possession and having won it, one or the other
turns with the ball to pass it to D. Alternatively, having turned
successfully, the winning player dribbles the ball over the line behind
him. The losing player can still recover to tackle or challenge for
possession.

It is important to understand the difference between a shoulder charge
and a push. It is almost impossible to push an opponent with the shoulder unless the charging player allows his arm and particularly his elbow to
move away from his side. Use of the arm constitutes a push or even worse
'striking an opponent'; the punishment for either can be very severe, especially in the penalty area!

5.58 Goalkeeping.

Increasingly, in modern soccer, the goalkeeper needs many of the techniques of an outfield player in addition to his specialist skills. He is often
required to play the part of a 'sweeper', a player deployed behind back
markers to cover them against any possibility of attacking break through.
To do this the goalkeeper is often positioned well outside the safety of his
own penalty area inside which, of course, he can handle the ball.

(a) Catching, Deflecting and Punching.

The different ways of catching, handling and holding a soccer ball
have been well described many times and will not be repeated here.
The important principle is security; the precautions taken in anticipation of a goalkeeper misjudgment. Some part of the goalkeeper's body
or head must be behind his hands and therefore behind the ball at the
moment of contact whenever possible.

When catching overhead, when jumping or when diving, it is not
immediately possible to set up secondary protection. Nevertheless,
the goalkeeper must draw the ball into the safety of his stomach or
upper body as soon as possible.

Catching the ball is simply another stopping skill along with an out
field player's chest control, thigh control, instep control and so on. The
principles for those skills are transferable to those of a goalkeeper.

(a) Whenever possible the body, or some part of it, must be directly
facing the ball's line of flight.

(b) The goalkeeper's feet must be on the move whenever he looks like being called to act.

(c) The stopping surfaces must be relaxed and withdrawn slightly before impact and continued after impact to absorb the force of the ball.

(d) The goalkeeper may be deceived by the movement of the ball through the air or off the ground; the ball may be deflected off another player. Not least, an opponent may feel that he has a good chance of reaching the ball before it reaches the goalkeeper which may cause a collision.

The goalkeeper's visual concentration must be on stopping, catching or deflecting the ball to safety.

Good strikers, like all predators, wait patiently for opportunities and they take them quickly.

Practices.
(1) Area: 10 yds x 10
Goals: 2 of a size to suit the age and development level of the practicing players.
The players 'feed' each other thrown services at the heights at which they require practice in catching or deflecting. The players should aim to catch the ball with their feet immediately beneath its line of flight or as near to that position as possible. Goalkeepers need 'fast feet'.

(2) Area: 20 yds x 30 yards divided into 3 zones each 10 yards deep.
Goals: 2
Players: A goalkeeper and one attacker in each end zone; 2 v 2 in the mid-zone and 1 floater who is always 'with' the attacking side.

Conditions: The mid-zone players pass the ball by throwing and catching until one can throw (or kick out of hands) to reach his team's goalkeeper.
A successful catch scores 1 point. Failure to hold the ball loses 1 point.
The single attacker can try to put the goalkeeper off and can challenge for any dropped catch or deflection. He can also intercept throws to the keeper to score. If the attacker scores, his team gains 2 points.
Following an attack, the game is restarted by centering the ball. Each mid-zone player stands in his own end zone. On a signal they race to the ball to restart the practice.

(b) Deflecting.
Principles.

A goalkeeper often can't catch safely and must deflect the ball to safety which usually means away from or over the goal and out of play. He may have to call on these skills having jumped to full stretch, horizontally or vertically. Full stretch means that he can only use one hand to deflect the ball; not many goalkeepers are able to catch the ball one handed: at least not in mid air!

Deflection is achieved using the fingered part of the palm. The movement possible at the joint between the fingers and the palm of the hand enable a goalkeeper to exert some directional control over the force of a shot. Where the shot is extremely powerful, a goalkeeper will try to deflect more with his palm than his fingers, resistance using his palm is greater than the strength of his fingers may allow. Goalkeepers need special arm, wrist and hand (fingers) strength training.

Deflection not only diverts shots wide of the target, it ensures that problem crosses are palmed safely over the crossbar and out of an attacker's reach.

Practices:

(1) In threes A throws to B who, using two hands or one, deflects the throw backwards and overhead to C. C jumps to catch or stands to 'field' the ball using goalkeeeping techniques to do so.

(2) In fours, the practice situation in (a) is repeated but D stands in front of B, but cannot interfere directly with B's jump and deflection. Not yet! Later he may jump with B trying to deflect with his head. This 4 player practice can be used to simulate play coming from the wings whereby the goalkeeper has to deflect the ball as far as possible behind him or over an imaginary crossbar out of play.

(3) In threes, A and C have a ball each. They serve alternately to B at heights which enable him to have repeated practice at catching or deflecting the ball in specific ways.

(4) Progression from (3) involves an opposing player representing an attacker. Initially this player can move about to disconcert B but he cannot interfere directly. Later he can jump to pretend to head any high services. Later still he can allow the ball to flick off any part of his body thereby testing B's reactions to surprise interventions.

(c) Diving to Catch or Deflect.
Principles.

Diving to save, to the side, high or low down is not so much a matter of getting airborne as a matter of landing safely. The force of landing is broken by using the whole forearm to absorb the shock which would be generated by a full body landing. Some goalkeepers, having dived to catch the ball, use it and the lower forearm to take the shock. The difficulty is in holding on to the ball in these circumstances. Landing shock moves down the player's body as each part hits the ground. It is likely to shake the ball out of the goalkeeper's grasp unless he pulls the ball into his stomach as soon as the first landing contact has been made. Control of the ball will be assisted if he can roll with the direction of his dive in a half curled position with the ball held securely within the curl.

As with all soccer techniques which may have painful consequences, players should be introduced to the full technique gradually and progressively, preferably in soft landing conditions.

(1) A serves the ball to B who, sitting, catches the ball. The service angle is widened until the goalkeeper has to fall sideways to catch the ball. Holding the ball as his lower arm contacts the ground is vital.

Progression: The player catches the serves from kneeling positions, first on both knees then on one. Practice progresses via kneeling to crouching and then to half standing at which time the goalkeeper has to fall to save and hold the ball.

Finally he is drawn into a full dive.

(2) Crab Soccer.
Area: 40 yds x 40
Goals: One on each side of the area 8 yds wide, with markers placed 2 yards inside each main goal post. The ball must never rise above knee height.
Balls: 1 or 2

4 v 4 and a goalkeeper defends each goal. A goal scored counts 2 points but a goal scored through a side goal (2 yards wide) scores 5 points.

The ball can be passed or a shot taken only by using the fist or the palm of the hand to strike the ball along the ground. A player cannot be prevented from passing the ball or shooting but passes and shots can be intercepted by diving, deflecting and so on. A ball is in possession when it is held in both hands. Players must move about the practice area on 'all fours'.

(3) Area: 10 yds x 10
Goals: Two, 8 yds wide. Each goal has a marker 2 yds inside each goal post.
Players: 2 goalkeepers, 1 attacker, two or more retrievers.
Balls: 2

Each goalkeeper throws or kicks in a predetermined way to score against his opponent. The single attacker waits for any goalkeeper mis-judgment which may allow him a shot. A goal scored through a mini goal scores 5 points. A goal scored through the larger goal scores 1 point.

Every fifth attack say, the single attacker should attempt to score by dribbling round the goalkeeper. This kind of goal scores 1 point.

(d) Diving at Opponents' Feet.
Principles.

When an opponent breaks clear with the ball, a goalkeeper must mini-mize the target. He moves out towards his opponent to present the largest possible barrier to his opponent. If his opponent approaches goal at an angle, a goalkeeper can present him with what from the attacker's view point seems a very small target indeed.

The goalkeeper needs to delay the opponent's shot until he can dive at the ball and at his opponent's feet. He dives to place his hands, arms and upper body, in that order, behind the ball. If he has 'read' the attacker's intentions accurately, the goalkeeper may catch the ball and use his upper forearm or hand to block the opponent's kicking leg before it develops full power.

The attacker is allowed to kick the ball until it is in the goalkeeper's pos-session but a quick moving, intelligent goalkeeper should be able to block even a shot taken very late; in fact the ball itself can be used as a shock absorber if the goalkeeper can get his vulnerable 'parts' behind the ball in time. If he can't, he has problems!

Practices.
(1) A walks or jogs with the ball towards goalkeeper B. A's moves should be without deception at this stage. B spreads himself, while moving forward, to present a barrier at A's feet and to grasp the ball. Having caught the ball A draws it into his curled body as quickly as possible.

The practice progresses with A trying to chip the ball over B as he goes down on the ball.

Later A can try to chip the ball over B or dribble the ball round him.

(2) Area: 40 yds x 30 with a 40 yds x 20 area marked off representing the penalty area.

Players: 1 goalkeeper, 1 feeder, 2 or 3 attackers, 1 retriever.

A serves the ball to an attacker in a variety of ways, allowing the attacker to collect the ball early and run on to attack the goal or to receive the pass with limited time to choose what action to take.

The attacker must dribble or shoot. Initially he will do more of one than of the other to give the goalkeeper specific practice by limiting his own options. The two or three attackers will approach goal from different angles in turn.

(e) Crosses and Corner Kicks.
Principles.

These situations involve catching, deflecting or punching the ball, often under severe opposing pressure and at optimum jumping height. Goalkeeper difficulties arise first from the length of time taken by the ball in flight and therefore the time available for opposing players to move to attack it.

Secondly the goalkeeper has to move to collect the ball at optimum jumping height coming from one direction while trying to anticipate the attempts by opponents to attack the ball from another direction; sometimes from behind him.

Finally the goalkeeper is hindered by the sheer number of players, his own and others, milling about the penalty area. Even if the ball is cleared it is likely to fall to an opponent who will try to shoot through a crowded area. The goalkeeper will have difficulty in sighting the shot as early as he would like.

Practices.

(1) At one end of a normal pitch, four players.

A throws the ball across the practice goal, imaginary or real. B, an opponent, can move wherever and whenever he wishes but cannot directly challenge for the ball unless the goalkeeper drops it.

Goalkeeper C catches the ball or deflects it powerfully as far as possible behind him. D is another server and the practice is repeated in the opposite direction.

Progression: Add one or two attackers and one defender. The goalkeeper and/or his co-defender attack the throw (or a volley out of the server's hands) aimed at space above the two attackers. The attackers stand still at first, then walk about and finally move about naturally but they cannot jump for the ball at this stage. The goalkeeper and the other defender must run through opponents and adjust take-off positions accordingly.

Further progression could allow both attackers and defenders to head the ball to other attackers to shoot through the cluster of players. Here, the goalkeeper doesn't jump for the ball but moves to locate possible strikers before they actually hit the ball.

(2) Catching the ball or deflecting it away from goal may not be safe enough options; the goalkeeper may have to punch the ball away. Punching is a difficult skill; it requires a goalkeeper to make very early decisions about his intentions.

Punching usually has to be done with one fist. If a goalkeeper can punch the ball with both fists together, the decision to punch may have been the wrong one; perhaps he should have caught the ball!

A goalkeeper uses an over arm swing to generate optimum punching power at the required height. As with all striking skills it is the speed of the fist at the moment of impact and the length of time the fist is in contact with the ball that generates power and therefore distance. Committed to jumping to punch the ball, a goalkeeper must be totally focused on contacting the ball to maximum effect; anyone in his way might be better out of it!

(3) Goalkeeper A stands behind B an attacker. C serves fairly high above B's head who remains stationary. A jumps to punch the ball clear of the penalty area to D. The practice progresses so that A receives a throw from a wide position and must now turn to punch sideways to a fourth player E.

(4) Area:40 yds x 40
Goals: At each end, 8 yds wide or as required.
Teams: 3 v 3 with 1 'floating' player always with the attacking team.
Each team has a goalkeeper.

Conditions: No player is allowed to run when holding the ball.
All passes must be above head height.

Teams progress to shooting positions by handball sequences of throw and catch. Within three paces of goal the attacking team may take a free throw to any player to run and head for goal. The attacking side always has a floating player advantage so at least one player will be unmarked for a free header.

Practices: (1) to (4) can be adapted to emphasize the 'fielding' and catching techniques for shots at most levels.

(f) Throwing.
Principles.
The three basic methods of throwing the ball for goalkeepers are:

(1) The over-arm throw:
(2) The spear or javelin throw and
(3) the underarm or 'bowling' throw as it is known in England.

A side arm slinging action is used by some goalkeepers but sacrifices control for power: the ball can finish up anywhere almost.

The first method can produce considerable elevation as the ball leaves the player's hand. The length of the throwing arm enables the 'keeper to generate exceptional power. Some goalkeepers can throw the ball almost as far as they can kick it. The problem, when aiming for optimum distance, is the time taken to 'wind up' into the throwing action and the effort involved. Time gives opponents a chance of intercepting and of moving a long way to do so.

The spear or javelin throw allows for optimum power over a relatively short distance although there are very strong goalkeepers who can achieve accuracy over 40 yards. This technique uses a much flatter trajectory than the over-arm method; the ball travels from hand to the receiver's feet more or less in a straight line. Problems arise for young players who haven't the hand size necessary to hold the ball from the 'wind up' through the long, fast, throwing movement from behind the body to the point of release.

The third method is used only over short distances, five to fifteen yards say, and to players who expect to receive and control the ball with the fewest problems and who could be in serious trouble if they don't! The underarm 'bowling' action is safe, easy to accomplish and since the ball is on the ground from the moment it leaves the goalkeeper's hand, control presents the receiver with no problems.

Practices.
(1) Area: 40 yds x 40
Goal: 1
Players: 3 goalkeepers
Goalkeeper B receives a long, high kick from A. Having caught or fielded the ball, he throws out to C. Practice is then repeated in the other direction.

(1) Progression. Diagram 59.
Both the target players, C and D, start inside the shaded central areas. Both can move wide to call for and receive the throw. The goalkeeper makes the decision and occasionally practices changing his target. . . quickly.

An opponent, E, is introduced in a central position. As soon as the goalkeeper catches the service and the target players move to wide receiving

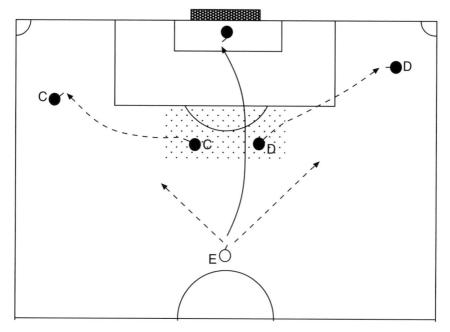

Diagram 59. *Players 'show' themselves for the goalkeeper's throws in 'wide' positions. An opponent may challenge to intercept the throw out.*

positions, E can move to get as close as possible to threaten one of the receivers. The goalkeeper must assess the direction of challenge quickly to decide which of the two will be his target.

(2) Further progression might involve the introduction of a forward striker who, while not interfering directly with the goalkeeper's actions, is there as a threat against any errors.

(3) Later, there may be three target players, 11, 5 and 7 and two opponents, black 9 and 10. Diagram 60. Black 9 and 10 must not leave the shaded area until the goalkeeper collects the service from S. They can then move freely to challenge for the ball. A target player, T, having received the 'keeper's throw, can pass up field to S, inter-pass with another player to pass upfield to S or pass back to the goalkeeper. Adding one or more players gradually to create an increasingly complex and therefore realistic picture is the hall mark of effective teaching.

The same organization and progression can be used for practicing the other throwing methods. The adjustment will be to the starting positions of receivers. When opponents are introduced, they will start from the two central shaded areas nearer to goal.

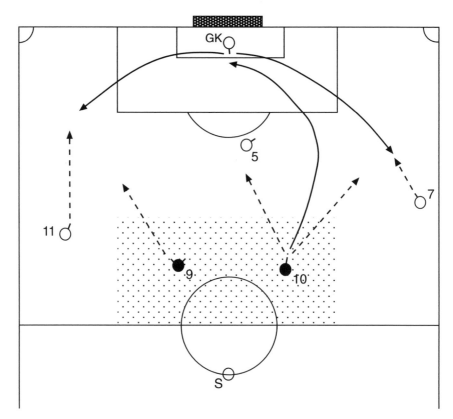

Diagram 60. *Goalkeepers select from three throw out options. Opponents 9 and 10 may challenge any of the three options. 'S' the server is the ultimate target for the three white players.*

(4) Area: 40 yds x 40
Goals: 2
Teams: 2 with four players each:
Floating player: 1
Balls: 1

The practice is started with a jump off in the centre. Whichever team wins, the ball must be passed back to that team's in-goal player (goalkeeper). One player from the opposing team must also drop back to become the temporary goalkeeper. The floating player always plays for the team which has possession of the ball. This creates a permanent 4 v 3 attacking situation. The goalkeeper in possession now selects a target player for his throws. 1 point is scored by passing the ball to the opposing goalkeeper who must catch it. If he allows the ball to cross the goal line he concedes 3 points.

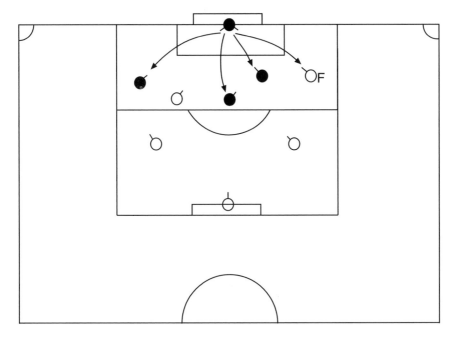

Diagram 61. *'Throw Outs', 4 v 4 Practice.*

(5) Ground Handball. Diagram 61.
Area: 40 yds x 40.
Goals: 2, each five yards wide.
Teams: Two teams of 5 players; each team has a nominated goalkeeper and his team attacks towards him. The goalkeeper can be changed at any time by notifying the referee.

The ball is passed underarm or using the javelin throw. The ball must travel along the ground or it must strike the ground (or bounce) before reaching a pass receiver, including the goalkeeper. A goal is scored by throwing the ball to the goalkeeper who must be on his goal line. To increase difficulty a close marker is used against a goalkeeper.

Conclusion

Every young player should be given experience at playing as a back defender, as a sweeper behind the backs, as a midfield player, as a striker, both wide and central, and as a goalkeeper. Soccer players born to play in this position or that are a figment of imagination. Teachers try (or should try) to give youngsters the broadest possible perspective of what is being taught. Experience is invaluable in later life and all aspects of human endeavor expand and grow on the basis of applied experience. Soccer is no exception.

Specialization should only assume importance when achievement in sport, in soccer or in life generally is accorded considerable significance. We as a society may be in danger of attaching too much significance to achievement by very young sports people too soon. Soccer throughout the world faces that danger. Teachers should resist such trends, they are not in a child's best interests nor, if we think about it, are they in the interests of society.

Teachers must stand up to be counted on this issue.

This book is for teachers, not for those who see themselves as puppet masters: people who pull the strings by which young players are expected to jerk, twitch and play as their masters command: have nothing to do with them.

Other books from **REEDSWAIN**

Allen Wade's other NEW Books.

PRINCIPLES OF
Effective
Coaching
#245 • $14.95

POSITIONAL PLAY
Back
Defenders
#2531: • $12.95

POSITIONAL PLAY
Midfield
#2532: • $12.95

POSITIONAL PLAY
Strikers
#2533: • $12.95

POSITIONAL PLAY
Goalkeeping
#2534: • $12.95

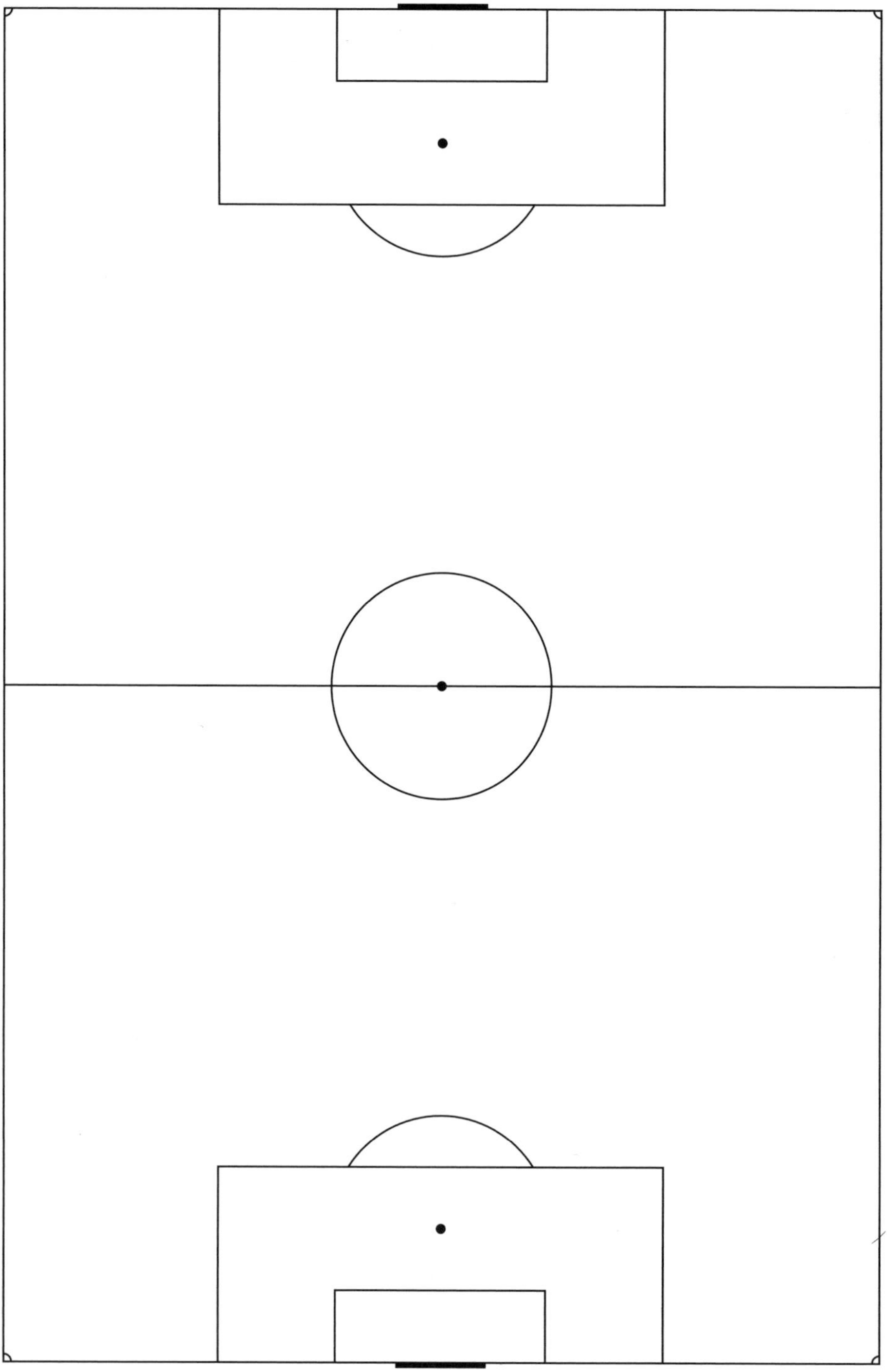

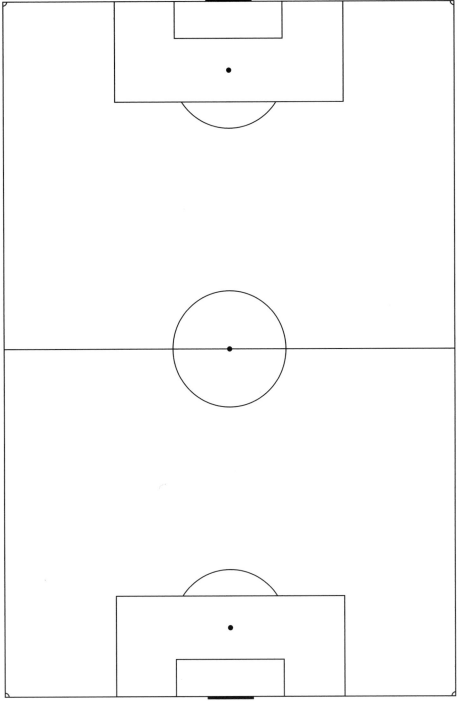

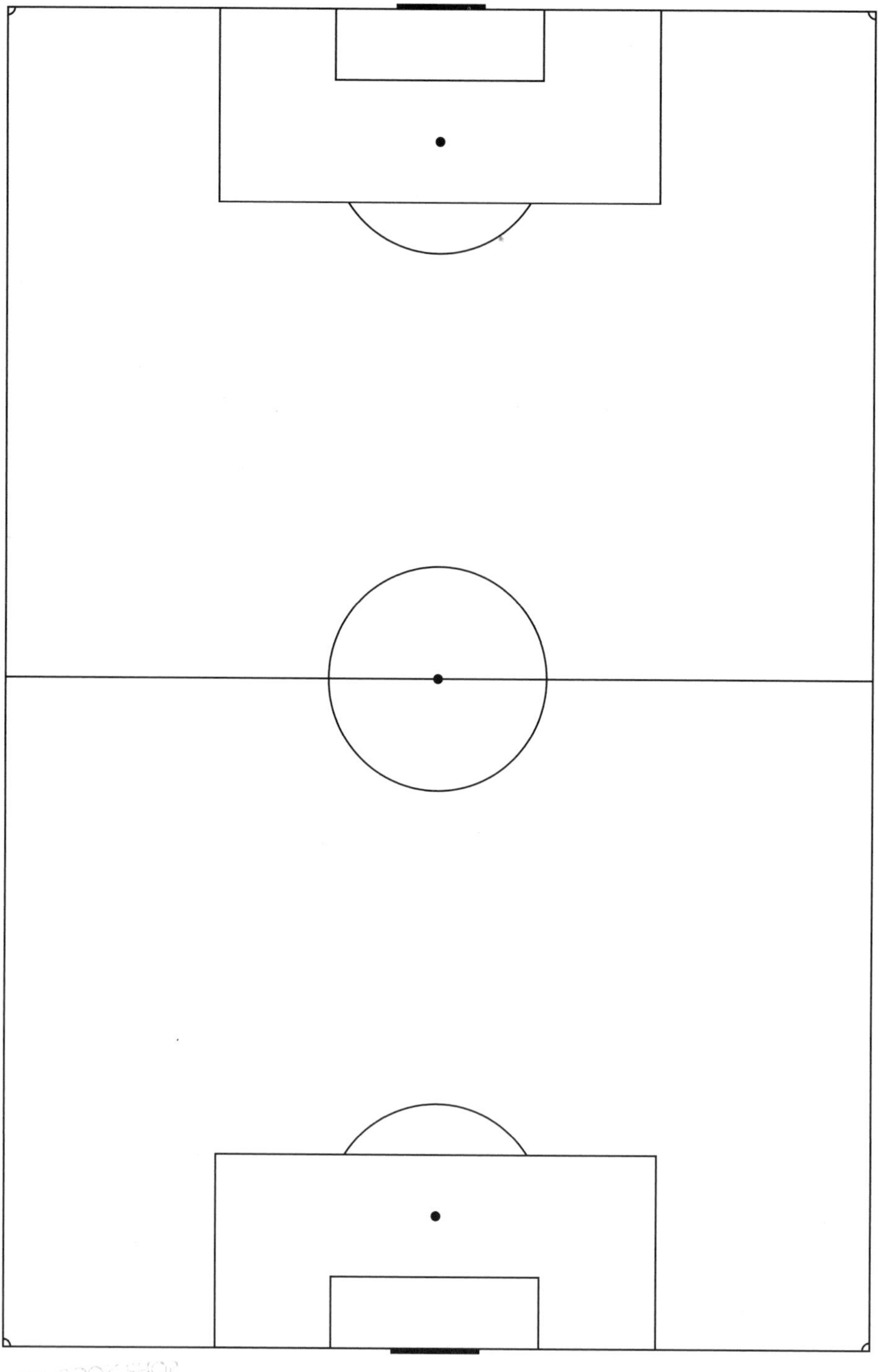